POEMS FOR TORTURED SOULS

Little, Brown and Company
Hachette Book Group
1290 Avenue of the Americas, New York, NY 10104
Visit us at LBYR.com

Originally published in the UK by Hodder & Stoughton in June 2024
First US Edition: September 2024

Little, Brown and Company is a division of Hachette Book Group, Inc. The Little, Brown
name and logo are registered trademarks of Hachette Book Group, Inc.

The publisher is not responsible for websites (or their content) that are not owned by the
publisher.

Little, Brown and Company books may be purchased in bulk for business, educational,
or promotional use. For information, please contact your local bookseller or the Hachette
Book Group Special Markets Department at special.markets@hbgusa.com.

ISBN 978-0-316-58414-2

Printed in Indiana, USA

LSC-C

Printing 1, 2024

POEMS FOR TORTURED SOULS

Selected by

Liz Ison

Little, Brown and Company
New York Boston

Contents

Introduction 7

Love 9

Heartache 39

Revenge 73

Folklore 109

Peace 151

Author Biographies 181

A Playlist for Tortured Souls 192

Dear Reader,

Writing songs, lyrics, and poetry can help us sort through our feelings and free our creativity. Maybe that's what Taylor Swift had in mind when she said making music was a "lifeline" for her. Many of us— during intense times—turn to our favorite artists, or to poets, to help us find the words and thoughts that we might have trouble expressing ourselves.

In that spirit, here is a collection of poems for those heightened moments, when we are looking for the words to make sense of our experiences or when we are searching for a way of connecting. These poems have traveled to you from far and wide. From England to New England, and from over hundreds of years of history. But wherever and whenever they originated, the words of these great poems resonate here and now. They might even inspire you to write your own songs or poetry.

Poems for Tortured Souls inhabits a space where inner and outer worlds collide and describes the paradox of relationships that make us feel so alone. These tortured poets tell of experiences that are individual yet universal, and that explore the connections between the past, the present, and an uncertain future. Here we rest momentarily in the borderlands—emotionally complex and haunting soundscapes created from the stories of our collective imagination.

I invite you to explore the different eras of tortured poetry—Love, Heartache, Revenge, Folklore, and Peace—and to make friends with these timeless verses, some written by poets who Taylor Swift has referenced in her own writing. As William Wordsworth, one of the Lake poets, foreshadowed in his *Prelude*, I wish you "all powers of swiftness, subtilty and strength"!

Yours fearlessly,

Liz Ison

Love

/luv/ – noun

A strong and positive emotional state.
To like someone so much that their happiness
is important to you.

A Red, Red Rose
Robert Burns

O my Luve is like a red, red rose
    That's newly sprung in June;
O my Luve is like the melody
    That's sweetly played in tune.

So fair art thou, my bonnie lass,
    So deep in luve am I;
And I will luve thee still, my dear,
    Till a' the seas gang dry.

Till a' the seas gang dry, my dear,
    And the rocks melt wi' the sun;
I will love thee still, my dear,
    While the sands o' life shall run.

And fare thee weel, my only luve!
    And fare thee weel awhile!
And I will come again, my luve,
    Though it were ten thousand mile.

You! Inez!

Alice Moore Dunbar-Nelson

Orange gleams athwart a crimson soul
Lambent flames; purple passion lurks
In your dusk eyes.
Red mouth; flower soft,
Your soul leaps up—and flashes
Star-like, white, flame-hot.
Curving arms, encircling a world of love,
You! Stirring the depths of passionate desire!

One Sister have I in our house

Emily Dickinson

One Sister have I in our house,
And one a hedge away,
There's only one recorded
But both belong to me.

One came the way that I came
And wore my past year's gown,
The other as a bird her nest,
Builded our hearts among.

She did not sing as we did,
It was a different tune,
Herself to her a music
As Bumble-bee of June.

To-day is far from childhood
But up and down the hills
I held her hand the tighter,
Which shortened all the miles.

And still her hum the years among
Deceives the Butterfly,
Still in her eye the Violets lie
Mouldered this many May.

I spilt the dew but took the morn,
I chose this single star
From out the wide night's numbers,
Sue—forevermore!

EMILY.

"Come, night, come Romeo"
William Shakespeare

From **ROMEO AND JULIET, Act III, Scene II**

Come, night, come Romeo; come, thou day in night;
For thou wilt lie upon the wings of night
Whiter than new snow upon a raven's back.
Come gentle night, come loving black-brow'd night,
Give me my Romeo, and when I shall die,
Take him and cut him out in little stars,
And he will make the face of heaven so fine
That all the world will be in love with night,
And pay no worship to the garish sun.
O, I have bought the mansion of a love,
But not possess'd it; and though I am sold,
Not yet enjoy'd. So tedious is this day
As is the night before some festival
To an impatient child that hath new robes
And may not wear them.

"How Do I Love Thee?"

Elizabeth Barrett Browning

How do I love thee? Let me count the ways.
I love thee to the depth and breadth and height
My soul can reach, when feeling out of sight
For the ends of Being and ideal Grace.
I love thee to the level of everyday's
Most quiet need, by sun and candlelight.
I love thee freely, as men strive for Right;
I love thee purely, as they turn from Praise.
I love thee with the passion put to use
In my old griefs, and with my childhood's faith.
I love thee with a love I seemed to lose
With my lost saints,—I love thee with the breath,
Smiles, tears, of all my life!—and, if God choose,
I shall but love thee better after death.

Romance

Claude McKay

To clasp you now and feel your head close-pressed,
Scented and warm against my beating breast;

To whisper soft and quivering your name,
And drink the passion burning in your frame;

To lie at full length, taut, with cheek to cheek,
And tease your mouth with kisses till you speak

Love words, mad words, dream words, sweet senseless
   words,
Melodious like notes of mating birds;

To hear you ask if I shall love always,
And myself answer: Till the end of days;

To feel your easeful sigh of happiness
When on your trembling lips I murmur: Yes;

It is so sweet. We know it is not true.
What matters it? The night must shed her dew.

We know it is not true, but it is sweet—
The poem with this music is complete.

Spring Rain

Sara Teasdale

I thought I had forgotten,
    But it all came back again
To-night with the first spring thunder
    In a rush of rain.

I remembered a darkened doorway
    Where we stood while the storm swept by,
Thunder gripping the earth
    And lightning scrawled on the sky.

The passing motor busses swayed,
    For the street was a river of rain,
Lashed into little golden waves
    In the lamp light's stain.

With the wild spring rain and thunder
    My heart was wild and gay;
Your eyes said more to me that night
    Than your lips would ever say....

I thought I had forgotten,
    But it all came back again
To-night with the first spring thunder
    In a rush of rain.

An Hour with Thee

Sir Walter Scott

An hour with thee!—When earliest day
Dapples with gold the eastern grey,
Oh, what can frame my mind to bear
The toil and turmoil, cark and care,
New griefs, which coming hours unfold
And sad remembrance of the old?

One hour with thee!

One hour with thee! When burning June
Waves his red flag at pitch of noon,
What shall repay the faithful swain,
His labour on the sultry plain,
And, more than cave or sheltering bough,
Cool feverish blood, and throbbing brow?—

One hour with thee!

One hour with thee!—When sun is set,
O, what can teach me to forget
The thankless labours of the day;
The hopes, the wishes, flung away;
The increasing wants, and lessening gains,
The master's pride who scorns my pains?

One hour with thee!

"I wish I could remember that first day"

Christina Rossetti

I wish I could remember that first day,
First hour, first moment of your meeting me,
If bright or dim the season, it might be
Summer or Winter for aught I can say;
So unrecorded did it slip away,
So blind was I to see and to foresee,
So dull to mark the budding of my tree
That would not blossom yet for many a May.
If only I could recollect it, such
A day of days! I let it come and go
As traceless as a thaw of bygone snow;
It seemed to mean so little, meant so much;
If only now I could recall that touch,
First touch of hand in hand—Did one but know!

"With thee conversing
I forget all time"
John Milton

From **PARADISE LOST, BOOK IV**

Eve speaks to Adam

With thee conversing I forget all time;
All seasons, and their change, all please alike.
Sweet is the breath of Morn, her rising sweet,
With charm of earliest birds: pleasant the sun,
When first on this delightful land he spreads
His orient beams, on herb, tree, fruit, and flower,
Glistering with dew; fragrant the fertile earth
After soft showers; and sweet the coming on
Of grateful Evening mild; then silent Night
With this her solemn bird and this fair moon,
And these the gems of Heaven, her starry train:
But neither breath of Morn when she ascends
With charm of earliest birds; nor rising sun
On this delightful land, nor herb, fruit, flower,
Glistering with dew; nor fragrance after showers;
Nor grateful Evening mild; nor silent Night
With this her solemn bird; nor walk by moon,
Or glittering star-light without thee is sweet

Invitation to Love
Paul Laurence Dunbar

Come when the nights are bright with stars
   Or come when the moon is mellow;
Come when the sun his golden bars
   Drops on the hay-field yellow.
Come in the twilight soft and gray,
Come in the night or come in the day,
Come, O love, whene'er you may,
   And you are welcome, welcome.

You are sweet, O Love, dear Love,
You are soft as the nesting dove.
Come to my heart and bring it rest
As the bird flies home to its welcome nest.

Come when my heart is full of grief
   Or when my heart is merry;
Come with the falling of the leaf
   Or with the redd'ning cherry.
Come when the year's first blossom blows,
Come when the summer gleams and glows,
Come with the winter's drifting snows,
   And you are welcome, welcome.

A Decade

Amy Lowell

When you came, you were like red wine and honey,
And the taste of you burnt my mouth with its
    sweetness.
Now you are like morning bread,
Smooth and pleasant.
I hardly taste you at all for I know your savour,
But I am completely nourished.

"My True Love Hath My Heart"

Sir Philip Sidney

My true-love hath my heart, and I have his,
By just exchange, one for the other given:
I hold his dear, and mine he cannot miss;
There never was a bargain better driven.

His heart in me keeps me and him in one;
My heart in him his thoughts and senses guides:
He loves my heart for once it was his own;
I cherish his because in me it bides.

His heart his wound received from my sight;
My heart was wounded, with his wounded heart;
For as from me on him his hurt did light,
So still, methought, in me his hurt did smart:
Both equal hurt, in this change sought our bliss,
My true love hath my heart and I have his.

One Day I Wrote her Name

Edmund Spenser

One day I wrote her name upon the strand,
But came the waves and washed it away:
Again I wrote it with a second hand,
But came the tide, and made my pains his prey.
"Vain man," said she, "that dost in vain assay,
A mortal thing so to immortalize;
For I myself shall like to this decay,
And eke my name be wiped out likewise."
"Not so," (quod I) "let baser things devise
To die in dust, but you shall live by fame:
My verse your vertues rare shall eternize,
And in the heavens write your glorious name:
Where whenas death shall all the world subdue,
Our love shall live, and later life renew."

Union Square

Sara Teasdale

With the man I love who loves me not,
 I walked in the street-lamps' flare;
We watched the world go home that night
 In a flood through Union Square.

I leaned to catch the words he said
 That were light as a snowflake falling;
Ah well that he never leaned to hear
 The words my heart was calling.

And on we walked and on we walked
 Past the fiery lights of the picture shows—
Where the girls with thirsty eyes go by
 On the errand each man knows.

And on we walked and on we walked,
 At the door at last we said good-bye;
I knew by his smile he had not heard
 My heart's unuttered cry.

With the man I love who loves me not
 I walked in the street-lamps' flare—
But oh, the girls who ask for love
 In the lights of Union Square.

The Hawthorn Tree

Willa Cather

Across the shimmering meadows—
Ah, when he came to me!
In the spring-time,
In the night-time,
In the starlight,
Beneath the hawthorn tree.

Up from the misty marsh-land—
Ah, when he climbed to me!
To my white bower,
To my sweet rest,
To my warm breast,
Beneath the hawthorn tree.

Ask of me what the birds sang,
High in the hawthorn tree;
What the breeze tells,
What the rose smells,
What the stars shine—
Not what he said to me!

Episode

Elsa Gidlow

I have robbed the garrulous streets,
Thieved a fair girl from their blight,
I have stolen her for a sacrifice
That I shall make to this mysteried night.

I have brought her, laughing,
To my quietly sinister garden.
For what will be done there
I ask no man's pardon.

I brush the rouge from her cheeks,
Clean the black kohl from the rims
Of her eyes; loose her hair;
Uncover the glimmering, shy limbs.

I break wild roses, scatter them over her.
The thorns between us sing like love's pain.
Her flesh, bitter and salt to my tongue,
I taste with endless kisses and taste again.

At dawn I leave her
Asleep in my wakening garden
(For what was done there
I ask no man's pardon.)

Free Love

Henry David Thoreau

My love must be as free
    As is the eagle's wing,
Hovering o'er land and sea
    And everything.

I must not dim my eye
    In thy saloon,
I must not leave my sky
    And nightly moon.

Be not the fowler's net
    Which stays my flight,
And craftily is set
    T' allure the sight,

But be the favoring gale
    That bears me on,
And still doth fill my sail
    When thou art gone.

I cannot leave my sky
    For thy caprice,
True love would soar as high
    As heaven is.

The eagle would not brook
  Her mate thus won,
Who trained his eye to look
  Beneath the sun.

Two Loves

Lucy Maud Montgomery

One said; 'Lo, I would walk hand-clasped with thee
Adown the ways of joy and sunlit slopes
Of earthly song in happiest vagrancy
To pluck the blossom of a thousand hopes.
Let us together drain the wide world's cup
With gladness brimméd up!'

And one said, 'I would pray to go with thee
When sorrow claims thee; I would fence thy heart
With mine against all anguish; I would be
The comforter and healer of thy smart;
And I would count it all the wide world's gain
To spare or share thy pain!'

Camomile Tea

Katherine Mansfield

Outside the sky is light with stars;
There's a hollow roaring from the sea.
And, alas! for the little almond flowers,
The wind is shaking the almond tree.

How little I thought, a year ago,
In the horrible cottage upon the Lee
That he and I should be sitting so
And sipping a cup of camomile tea.

Light as feathers the witches fly,
The horn of the moon is plain to see;
By a firefly under a jonquil flower
A goblin toasts a bumble-bee.

We might be fifty, we might be five,
So snug, so compact, so wise are we!
Under the kitchen-table leg
My knee is pressing against his knee.

Our shutters are shut, the fire is low,
The tap is dripping peacefully;
The saucepan shadows on the wall
Are black and round and plain to see.

Stanzas ("O, come to me in dreams, my love!")

Mary Wollstonecraft Shelley

O, come to me in dreams, my love!
  I will not ask a dearer bliss;
Come with the starry beams, my love,
  And press mine eyelids with thy kiss.

'Twas thus, as ancient fables tell,
  Love visited a Grecian maid,
Till she disturbed the sacred spell,
  And woke to find her hopes betrayed.

But gentle sleep shall veil my sight,
  And Psyche's lamp shall darkling be,
When, in the visions of the night,
  Thou dost renew thy vows to me.

Then come to me in dreams, my love,
  I will not ask a dearer bliss;
Come with the starry beams, my love,
  And press mine eyelids with thy kiss.

Absence

Claude McKay

Your words dropped into my heart like pebbles into a
    pool,
Rippling around my breast and leaving it melting cool.

Your kisses fell sharp on my flesh like dawn-dews from
    the limb,
Of a fruit-filled lemon tree when the day is young and
    dim.

Like soft rain-christened sunshine, as fragile as rare
    gold lace,
Your breath, sweet-scented and warm, has kindled my
    tranquil face.

But a silence vasty-deep, oh deeper than all these ties
Now, through the menacing miles, brooding between
    us lies.

And more than the songs I sing, I await your written
    word,
To stir my fluent blood as never your presence stirred.

Green

D. H. Lawrence

The dawn was apple-green,
The sky was green wine held up in the sun,
The moon was a golden petal between.

She opened her eyes, and green
They shone, clear like flowers undone
For the first time, now for the first time seen.

After Parting

Sara Teasdale

Oh I have sown my love so wide
   That he will find it everywhere;
It will awake him in the night,
   It will enfold him in the air.

I set my shadow in his sight
   And I have winged it with desire,
That it may be a cloud by day
   And in the night a shaft of fire.

"Since brass, nor stone, nor earth, nor boundless sea"
William Shakespeare

Sonnet 65

Since brass, nor stone, nor earth, nor boundless sea,
But sad mortality o'er-sways their power,
How with this rage shall beauty hold a plea
Whose action is no stronger than a flower?
O, how shall summer's honey breath hold out
Against the wrackful siege of battering days,
When rocks impregnable are not so stout,
Nor gates of steel so strong, but Time decays?
O fearful meditation! where, alack,
Shall Time's best jewel from Time's chest lie hid?
Or what strong hand can hold his swift foot back?
Or who his spoil of beauty can forbid?
    O, none, unless this miracle have might,
     That in black ink my love may still shine bright.

Wild nights—Wild nights!

Emily Dickinson

Wild nights! Wild nights!
Were I with thee,
Wild nights should be
Our luxury!

Futile the winds
To a heart in port,—
Done with the compass,
Done with the chart.

Rowing in Eden!
Ah! the sea!
Might I but moor
To-night in thee!

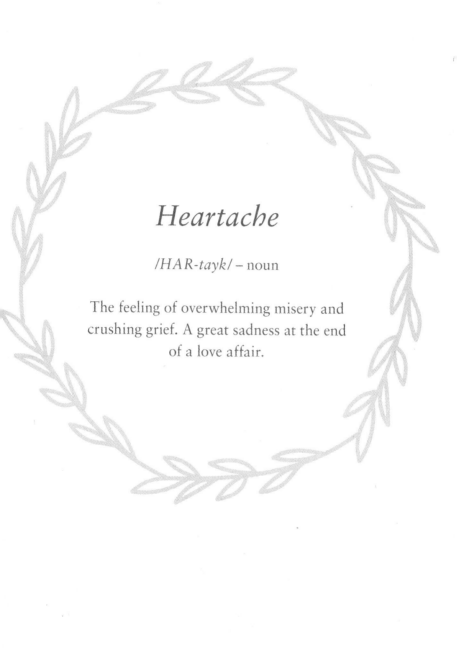

Heartache

/HAR-tayk/ – noun

The feeling of overwhelming misery and
crushing grief. A great sadness at the end
of a love affair.

Ebb

Edna St. Vincent Millay

I know what my heart is like
    Since your love died:
It is like a hollow ledge
Holding a little pool
    Left there by the tide,
    A little tepid pool,
Drying inward from the edge.

The Call

George Roberts

From the fireside of your heart
Where love blew the peats aglow,
I arise, I will depart,
I must go.

Peace was dwelling in your eyes,
But across my soft content,
Gleams like rays in midnight skies
Quivered and went.

I arise though blind with tears
To fare forth on the long way.
When the beckoning gleam appears
I must obey.

Twice

Christina Rossetti

Extract

I took my heart in my hand
   (O my love, O my love),
I said: Let me fall or stand,
   Let me live or die,
But this once hear me speak
   (O my love, O my love)—
Yet a woman's words are weak;
   You should speak, not I.

You took my heart in your hand
   With a friendly smile,
With a critical eye you scann'd,
   Then set it down,
And said, 'It is still unripe,
   Better wait awhile;
Wait while the skylarks pipe,
   Till the corn grows brown.'

As you set it down it broke—
   Broke, but I did not wince;
I smiled at the speech you spoke,
   At your judgement I heard:
But I have not often smiled
   Since then, nor question'd since,
Nor cared for cornflowers wild,
   Nor sung with the singing bird.

Pattern

Dorothy Parker

Leave me to my lonely pillow.
   Go, and take your silly posies;
Who has vowed to wear the willow
   Looks a fool, tricked out in roses.

Who are you, my lad, to ease me?
   Leave your pretty words unspoken.
Tinkling echoes little please me,
   Now my heart is freshly broken.

Over young are you to guide me,
   And your blood is slow and sleeping.
If you must, then sit beside me....
   Tell me, why have I been weeping?

Renouncement

Alice Meynell

I must not think of thee; and, tired yet strong,
    I shun the thought that lurks in all delight—
   The thought of thee—and in the blue Heaven's
      height,
And in the sweetest passage of a song.
Oh, just beyond the fairest thoughts that throng
   This breast, the thought of thee waits hidden
      yet bright;
   But it must never, never come in sight;
I must stop short of thee the whole day long.

But when sleep comes to close each difficult day,
   When night gives pause to the long watch I keep,
    And all my bonds I needs must loose apart,
Must doff my will as raiment laid away—
   With the first dream that comes with the first sleep
   I run, I run, I am gathered to thy heart.

"Time does not bring relief; you all have lied"

Edna St. Vincent Millay

Time does not bring relief; you all have lied
    Who told me time would ease me of my pain!
    I miss him in the weeping of the rain;
I want him at the shrinking of the tide;
The old snows melt from every mountain-side,
    And last year's leaves are smoke in every lane;
    But last year's bitter loving must remain
Heaped on my heart, and my old thoughts abide.

There are a hundred places where I fear
    To go,—so with his memory they brim!
And entering with relief some quiet place
Where never fell his foot or shone his face
I say, "There is no memory of him here!"
    And so stand stricken, so remembering him!

Poem (To F.S.)

Langston Hughes

I loved my friend.
He went away from me.
There's nothing more to say.
The poem ends,
Soft as it began,—
I loved my friend.

Sympathy

Paul Laurence Dunbar

I know what the caged bird feels, alas!
    When the sun is bright on the upland slopes;
When the wind stirs soft through the springing grass,
And the river flows like a stream of glass;
    When the first bird sings and the first bud opes,
And the faint perfume from its chalice steals—
I know what the caged bird feels!

I know why the caged bird beats his wing
    Till its blood is red on the cruel bars;
For he must fly back to his perch and cling
When he fain would be on the bough a-swing;
    And a pain still throbs in the old, old scars
And they pulse again with a keener sting—
I know why he beats his wing!

I know why the caged bird sings, ah me,
　　When his wing is bruised and his bosom sore,—
When he beats his bars and he would be free;
It is not a carol of joy or glee,
　　But a prayer that he sends from his heart's deep core,
But a plea, that upward to Heaven he flings—
I know why the caged bird sings!

"I wake and feel the fell of dark, not day"

Gerard Manley Hopkins

I wake and feel the fell of dark, not day.
What hours, O what black hours we have spent
This night! what sights you, heart, saw; ways you
    went!
And more must, in yet longer light's delay.

With witness I speak this. But where I say
Hours I mean years, mean life. And my lament
Is cries countless, cries like dead letters sent
To dearest him that lives alas! away.

I am gall, I am heartburn. God's most deep decree
Bitter would have me taste: my taste was me;
Bones built in me, flesh filled, blood brimmed the
    curse.

Selfyeast of spirit a dull dough sours. I see
The lost are like this, and their scourge to be
As I am mine, their sweating selves; but worse.

On Monsieur's Departure

Queen Elizabeth I

I grieve and dare not show my discontent,
I love and yet am forced to seem to hate,
I do, yet dare not say I ever meant,
I seem stark mute but inwardly do prate.
  I am and not, I freeze and yet am burned,
  Since from myself another self I turned.

My care is like my shadow in the sun,
Follows me flying, flies when I pursue it,
Stands and lies by me, doth what I have done.
His too familiar care doth make me rue it.
  No means I find to rid him from my breast,
  Till by the end of things it be supprest.

Some gentler passion slide into my mind,
For I am soft and made of melting snow;
Or be more cruel, love, and so be kind.
Let me or float or sink, be high or low.
  Or let me live with some more sweet content,
  Or die and so forget what love ere meant.

"I Am"
John Clare

1

I am—yet what I am, none cares or knows;
    My friends forsake me like a memory lost:—
I am the self-consumer of my woes;—
    They rise and vanish in oblivion's host,
Like shadows in love's frenzied stifled throes:—
And yet I am, and live—like vapours tost

2

Into the nothingness of scorn and noise,—
    Into the living sea of waking dreams,
Where there is neither sense of life or joys,
    But the vast shipwreck of my lifes esteems;
Even the dearest, that I love the best
Are strange—nay, rather stranger than the rest.

3

I long for scenes, where man hath never trod
    A place where woman never smiled or wept
There to abide with my Creator, God;
    And sleep as I in childhood, sweetly slept,
Untroubling, and untroubled where I lie,
The grass below—above the vaulted sky.

The Broken Field
Sara Teasdale

My soul is a dark ploughed field
   In the cold rain;
My soul is a broken field
   Ploughed by pain.

Where grass and bending flowers
   Were growing,
The field lies broken now
   For another sowing.

Great Sower when you tread
   My field again,
Scatter the furrows there
   With better grain.

The Parting

Ellen Johnston, also known as "The Factory Girl"

Farewell for ever, we must sever,
    I am no longer loved by thee;
I have been true, but thou may'st rue,
    The day thou didst prove false to me.

I thought the sun would cease to run
    His daily course around the sky,
Ere thou would'st prove a faithless lover,
    Or look on me with scornful eye.

Thy words were sweet when we did meet,
    I could not dream of secret guile,
Nor could I trace within thy face
    Deceit in thy dissembling smile.
This world's scorn is but a form —
    A fleeting phantom in my view,
I heed it not since thou hast brought
    A change o'er all the joys I knew.

Thou did'st impart joy to my heart,
    But now I feel the hope was vain;
'Twas but thy smile of treacherous guile
    That lighted up my dreaming brain.
I loved thee well; no tongue can tell
    The love I cherished up for thee;

I love thee still, despite thine ill.
    But Heaven alone my love shall see.

I will not blast the joy that's past,
    The happy hours I've spent with thee;
Nor yet estrange with deep revenge
    Thy love so falsely vowed to me.
Some chord may spring perchance to bring
    Thy memory back when first we meet;
Some conscious thought may mark the spot,
    And thou may'st feel some sad regret.

Some future hour of mystic power
    May bind thy mem'ry in a spell;
And thou may'st trace on time's iron face
    The wrongs that made my heart rebel.

My simple songs, my countless wrongs
    May swell before thee like a sea;
And thou may'st hate when it's too late
    All those that tried to injure me.

Perchance thy vow that's broken now,
    (All that on earth I once did cherish),
May come in dreams and midnight scenes,
    And waken guilt too strong to perish.
Adieu for ever! we must sever;
    Go. Thou art welcome, I am free;
Though falsehood's fame hath ting'd my name,
    Thou hast not proved its guilt in me.

The Lover's Appeal

Sir Thomas Wyatt

And wilt thou leave me thus?
Say nay! say nay! for shame,
To save thee from the blame
Of all my grief and grame.
And wilt thou leave me thus?
Say nay! say nay!

And wilt thou leave me thus,
That hath loved thee so long
In wealth and woe among:
And is thy heart so strong
As for to leave me thus?
Say nay! say nay!

And wilt thou leave me thus,
That hath given thee my heart
Never for to depart
Neither for pain nor smart:
And wilt thou leave me thus?
Say nay! say nay!

And wilt thou leave me thus,
And have no more pity
Of him that loveth thee?
Alas! thy cruelty!
And wilt thou leave me thus?
Say nay! say nay!

Donal Og ("Young Donal")

Lady Augusta Gregory

Translated from Gaelic: extract of an eighth-century
Irish ballad

It is late last night the dog was speaking of you;
the snipe was speaking of you in her deep marsh.
It is you are the lonely bird through the woods;
and that you may be without a mate until you find me.

You promised me, and you said a lie to me,
that you would be before me where the sheep are
    flocked;
I gave a whistle and three hundred cries to you,
and I found nothing there but a bleating lamb.

You promised me a thing that was hard for you,
a ship of gold under a silver mast;
twelve towns with a market in all of them,
and a fine white court by the side of the sea.

You promised me a thing that is not possible,
that you would give me gloves of the skin of a fish;
that you would give me shoes of the skin of a bird;
and a suit of the dearest silk in Ireland.

When I go by myself to the Well of Loneliness,
I sit down and I go through my trouble;
when I see the world and do not see my boy,
he that has an amber shade in his hair.

It was on that Sunday I gave my love to you;
the Sunday that is last before Easter Sunday.
And myself on my knees reading the Passion;
and my two eyes giving love to you for ever.

My mother said to me not to be talking with you
    to-day,
or to-morrow, or on the Sunday;
it was a bad time she took for telling me that;
it was shutting the door after the house was robbed.

My heart is as black as the blackness of the sloe,
or as the black coal that is on the smith's forge;
or as the sole of a shoe left in white halls;
it was you put that darkness over my life.

You have taken the east from me; you have taken the
    west from me;
you have taken what is before me and what is behind
    me;
you have taken the moon, you have taken the sun from
    me;
and my fear is great that you have taken God from me!

A Dream Within a Dream

Edgar Allan Poe

Take this kiss upon the brow!
And, in parting from you now,
Thus much let me avow—
You are not wrong, who deem
That my days have been a dream;
Yet if Hope has flown away
In a night, or in a day,
In a vision, or in none,
Is it therefore the less *gone*?
All that we see or seem
Is but a dream within a dream.

I stand amid the roar
Of a surf-tormented shore,
And I hold within my hand
Grains of the golden sand—
How few! yet how they creep
Through my fingers to the deep,
While I weep—while I weep!
O God! can I not grasp
Them with a tighter clasp?
O God! can I not save
One from the pitiless wave?
Is *all* that we see or seem
But a dream within a dream?

Since We Parted

Edward Robert Bulwer-Lytton

Since we parted yester-eve,
I do love thee, Love, believe,
Twelve times dearer, twelve hours longer,
One dream deeper, one night stronger,
One sun surer: thus much more
Than I loved thee, dear, before.

Evening Solace

Charlotte Brontë

The human heart has hidden treasures,
   In secret kept, in silence sealed;—
The thoughts, the hopes, the dreams, the pleasures,
   Whose charms were broken if revealed.
And days may pass in gay confusion,
   And nights in rosy riot fly,
While, lost in Fame's or Wealth's illusion,
   The memory of the Past may die.

But there are hours of lonely musing,
   Such as in evening silence come,
When, soft as birds their pinions closing,
   The heart's best feelings gather home.
Then in our souls there seems to languish
   A tender grief that is not woe;
And thoughts that once wrung groans of anguish
   Now cause but some mild tears to flow.

And feelings, once as strong as passions,
    Float softly back—a faded dream;
Our own sharp griefs and wild sensations,
    The tale of others' sufferings seem.
Oh! when the heart is freshly bleeding,
    How longs it for that time to be,
When, through the mist of years receding,
    Its woes but live in reverie!

And it can dwell on moonlight glimmer,
    On evening shade and loneliness;
And, while the sky grows dim and dimmer,
    Feel no untold and strange distress—
Only a deeper impulse given
    By lonely hour and darkened room,
To solemn thoughts that soar to heaven
    Seeking a life and world to come.

Ae Fond Kiss

Robert Burns

Ae fond kiss, and then we sever;
Ae fareweel, and then forever!
Deep in heart-wrung tears I'll pledge thee,
Warring sighs and groans I'll wage thee.
Who shall say that fortune grieves him,
While the star of hope she leaves him?
Me, nae cheerfu' twinkle lights me;
Dark despair around benights me.

I'll ne'er blame my partial fancy,
Naething could resist my Nancy;
But to see her was to love her;
Love but her, and love forever.
Had we never lov'd sae kindly,
Had we never lov'd sae blindly,
Never met—or never parted,
We had ne'er been broken-hearted.

Fare-thee-weel, thou first and fairest!
Fare-thee-weel, thou best and dearest!
Thine be ilka joy and treasure,
Peace, enjoyment, love, and pleasure!
Ae fond kiss, and then we sever!
Ae fareweel, alas, for ever!
Deep in heart-wrung tears I'll pledge thee,
Warring sighs and groans I'll wage thee.

Her First Sorrow

Ameen Rihani

'T is but a score of hours when he didst swear
My sorrow and my joy to share.
  Despite the fates, fore'er ;
But now he's gone to cash again his lie ;
  Others his shame with me will wear,
        Why should I die?

Last night his lips my very feet didst burn ;
His kisses dropt, my love to earn,
  Whichever way he'd turn ;
But now he's gone another soul to rob,
  Another heart to lure and spurn,
        Why should I sob?

He did not kiss me when he said good-bye ;
I let him go, not asking why,
  Nor do I for him sigh ;
He's gone another virgin breast to tear.
  He's gone on other lips to die,
        Why should I care?

Interim

Clarissa Scott Delany

The night was made for rest and sleep,
For winds that softly sigh;
It was not made for grief and tears;
So then why do I cry?

The wind that blows through leafy trees
Is soft and warm and sweet;
For me the night is a gracious cloak
To hide my soul's defeat.

Just one dark hour of shaken depths,
Of bitter black despair—
Another day will find me brave,
And not afraid to dare.

If I can stop one heart from breaking

Emily Dickinson

If I can stop one heart from breaking,
I shall not live in vain;
If I can ease one life the aching,
Or cool one pain,
Or help one fainting robin
Unto his nest again,
I shall not live in vain.

Stanzas

Emily Brontë

Often rebuked, yet always back returning
   To those first feelings that were born with me,
And leaving busy chase of wealth and learning
   For idle dreams of things which cannot be:

To-day, I will seek not the shadowy region;
   Its unsustaining vastness waxes drear;
And visions rising, legion after legion,
   Bring the unreal world too strangely near.

I'll walk, but not in old heroic traces,
   And not in paths of high morality,
And not among the half-distinguished faces,
   The clouded forms of long-past history.

I'll walk where my own nature would be leading:
   It vexes me to choose another guide:
Where the grey flocks in ferny glens are feeding,
   Where the wild wind blows on the mountain side.

What have those lonely mountains worth revealing?
   More glory and more grief than I can tell:
The earth that wakes *one* human heart to feeling
   Can centre both the worlds of Heaven and Hell.

On Change of Weathers

Francis Quarles

And were it for thy profit, to obtain
All *Sunshine*? No vicissitude of *Rain*?
Thinkst thou, that thy laborious *Plough* requires
Not Winter *frosts*, as well as Summer *fires*?
There must be both: Sometimes these hearts of ours
Must have the sweet, the seasonable Showers
Of *Tears*; Sometimes, the Frost of chill *despair*
Makes our desired *sunshine* seem more *fair*:
Weathers that most oppose the Flesh and Blood,
Are such as help to make our *Harvest* good:
We may not choose, great *God*; it is thy *Task*:
We know not what to *have*; nor how to *ask*.

After Love
Sara Teasdale

There is no magic any more,
    We meet as other people do,
You work no miracle for me
    Nor I for you.

You were the wind and I the sea—
    There is no splendor any more,
I have grown listless as the pool
    Beside the shore.

But though the pool is safe from storm
    And from the tide has found surcease,
It grows more bitter than the sea,
    For all its peace.

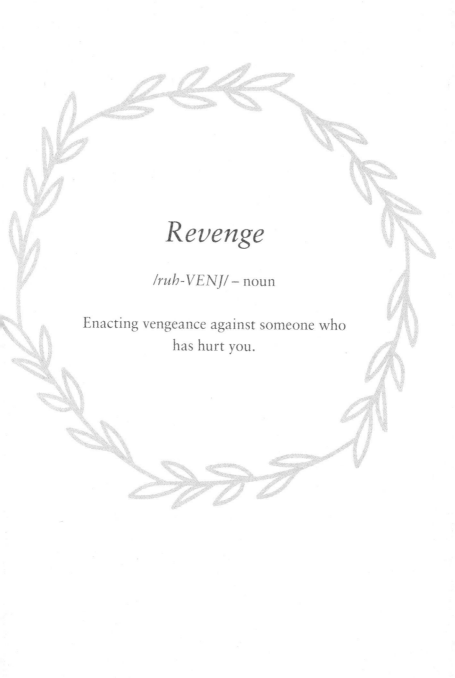

Revenge

/ruh-VENJ/ – noun

Enacting vengeance against someone who
has hurt you.

A Poison Tree
William Blake

I was angry with my friend:
I told my wrath, my wrath did end.
I was angry with my foe:
I told it not, my wrath did grow.

And I watered it in fears
Night and morning with my tears,
And I sunned it with smiles
And with soft deceitful wiles.

And it grew both day and night,
Till it bore an apple bright,
And my foe beheld it shine,
And he knew that it was mine,—

And into my garden stole
When the night had veiled the pole;
In the morning, glad, I see
My foe outstretched beneath the tree.

Carrefour

Amy Lowell

O You,
Who came upon me once
Stretched under apple-trees just after bathing,
Why did you not strangle me before speaking
Rather than fill me with the wild white honey of
    your words
And then leave me to the mercy
Of the forest bees.

"Two households, both alike in dignity"

William Shakespeare

From **ROMEO AND JULIET, The Prologue**

Two households, both alike in dignity,
In fair Verona, where we lay our scene,
From ancient grudge break to new mutiny,
Where civil blood makes civil hands unclean.
From forth the fatal loins of these two foes
A pair of star-cross'd lovers take their life;
Whose misadventur'd piteous overthrows
Doth with their death bury their parents' strife.
The fearful passage of their death-mark'd love,
And the continuance of their parents' rage,
Which, but their children's end, nought could remove,
Is now the two hours' traffic of our stage;
The which, if you with patient ears attend,
What here shall miss, our toil shall strive to mend.

Thought.
Alice Moore Dunbar-Nelson

A swift, successive chain of things,
That flash, kaleidoscope-like, now in, now out,
Now straight, now eddying in wild rings,
No order, neither law, compels their moves,
But endless, constant, always swiftly roves.

To My Enemy
Lucy Maud Montgomery

Let those who will of friendship sing,
    And to its guerdon grateful be,
But I a lyric garland bring
    To crown thee, O, mine enemy!

Thanks, endless thanks, to thee I owe
    For that my lifelong journey through
Thine honest hate has done for me
    What love perchance had failed to do.

I had not scaled such weary heights
    But that I held thy scorn in fear,
And never keenest lure might match
    The subtle goading of thy sneer.

Thine anger struck from me a fire
    That purged all dull content away,
Our mortal strife to me has been
    Unflagging spur from day to day.

And thus, while all the world may laud
    The gifts of love and loyalty,
I lay my meed of gratitude
    Before thy feet, mine enemy!

"For ivy climbs the crumbling hall"

Philip James Bailey

From **FESTUS**

For ivy climbs the crumbling hall
To decorate decay;
And spreads its dark deceitful pall
To hide what wastes away.

Apologia

Oscar Wilde

Is it thy will that I should wax and wane,
   Barter my cloth of gold for hodden grey,
And at thy pleasure weave that web of pain
   Whose brightest threads are each a wasted day?

Is it thy will—Love that I love so well—
   That my Soul's House should be a tortured spot
Wherein, like evil paramours, must dwell
   The quenchless flame, the worm that dieth not?

Nay, if it be thy will I shall endure,
   And sell ambition at the common mart,
And let dull failure be my vestiture,
   And sorrow dig its grave within my heart.

Perchance it may be better so—at least
   I have not made my heart a heart of stone,
Nor starved my boyhood of its goodly feast,
   Nor walked where Beauty is a thing unknown.

Many a man hath done so; sought to fence
   In straitened bonds the soul that should be free,
Trodden the dusty road of common sense,
   While all the forest sang of liberty,

Not marking how the spotted hawk in flight
　　Passed on wide pinion through the lofty air,
To where the steep untrodden mountain height
　　Caught the last tresses of the Sun God's hair.

Or how the little flower he trod upon,
　　The daisy, that white-feathered shield of gold,
Followed with wistful eyes the wandering sun
　　Content if once its leaves were aureoled.

But surely it is something to have been
　　The best belovèd for a little while,
To have walked hand in hand with Love, and seen
　　His purple wings flit once across thy smile.

Ay! though the gorgèd asp of passion feed
　　On my boy's heart, yet have I burst the bars,
Stood face to face with Beauty, known indeed
　　The Love which moves the Sun and all the stars!

Anger

Charles Lamb and Mary Lamb

Anger in its time and place
May assume a kind of grace.
It must have some reason in it,
And not last beyond a minute.
If to further lengths it go,
It does into malice grow.
'Tis the difference that we see
'Twixt the Serpent and the Bee.
If the latter you provoke,
It inflicts a hasty stroke,
Puts you to some little pain,
But it *never stings again*.
Close in tufted bush or brake
Lurks the poison-swelled snake,
Nursing up his cherished wrath.
In the purlieus of his path,
In the cold, or in the warm,
Mean him good, or mean him harm,
Whensoever fate may bring you,
The vile snake will *always sting you*.

A Thousand Martyrs

Aphra Behn

A thousand martyrs I have made,
   All sacrificed to my desire;
A thousand beauties have betrayed,
   That languish in resistless fire.
The untamed heart to hand I brought,
And fixed the wild and wandering thought.

I never vowed nor sighed in vain
   But both, though false, were well received.
The fair are pleased to give us pain,
   And what they wish is soon believed.
And though I talked of wounds and smart,
Love's pleasures only touched my heart.

Alone the glory and the spoil
   I always laughing bore away;
The triumphs, without pain or toil,
   Without the hell, the heav'n of joy.
And while I thus at random rove
Despise the fools that whine for love.

"I shot the ALBATROSS"

Samuel Taylor Coleridge

Extracts from **THE RIME OF THE ANCIENT MARINER**

From PART I

And now there came both mist
    and snow,
And it grew wondrous cold:
And ice, mast-high, came floating
    by,
As green as emerald.

*The land of ice, and of
fearful sounds, where
no living thing was to
be seen.*

And through the drifts the snowy
    clifts
Did send a dismal sheen:
Nor shapes of men nor beasts we
    ken—
The ice was all between.

The ice was here, the ice was
    there,
The ice was all around:
It cracked and growled, and
    roared and howled,
Like noises in a swound!

At length did cross an Albatross,
Thorough the fog it came;
As if it had been a Christian soul,
We hailed it in God's name.

It ate the food it ne'er had eat,
And round and round it flew.
The ice did split with a
    thunder-fit;
The helmsman steered us through!

And a good south wind sprung up
    behind;
The Albatross did follow,
And every day, for food or play,
Came to the mariner's hollo!

In mist or cloud, on mast or
    shroud,
It perched for vespers nine;
Whiles all the night, through
    fog-smoke white,
Glimmered the white Moon-shine.

"God save thee, ancient Mariner!
From the fiends, that plague thee
    thus!—
Why look'st thou so?"—With my
    cross-bow
I shot the ALBATROSS.

PART II

The Sun now rose upon the right:
Out of the sea came he,
Still hid in mist, and on the left
Went down into the sea.

And the good south wind still
    blew behind,
But no sweet bird did follow,
Nor any day for food or play
Came to the mariner's hollo!

His shipmates cry out against the ancient Mariner, for killing the bird of good luck.

And I had done a hellish thing,
And it would work 'em woe:
For all averred, I had killed the bird
That made the breeze to blow.
Ah wretch! said they, the bird to slay,
That made the breeze to blow!

But when the fog cleared off, they justify the same, and thus make themselves accomplices in the crime.

Nor dim nor red, like God's own head,
The glorious Sun uprist:
Then all averred, I had killed the bird
That brought the fog and mist.
'Twas right, said they, such birds to slay,
That bring the fog and mist.

The fair breeze continues; the ship enters the Pacific Ocean, and sails northward, even till it reaches the line.

The fair breeze blew, the white foam flew,
The furrow followed free;
We were the first that ever burst
Into that silent sea.

The ship hath been suddenly becalmed.

Down dropt the breeze, the sails
    dropt down,
'Twas sad as sad could be;
And we did speak only to break
The silence of the sea!

All in a hot and copper sky,
The bloody Sun, at noon,
Right up above the mast did
    stand,
No bigger than the Moon.

Day after day, day after day,
We stuck, nor breath nor
    motion;
As idle as a painted ship
Upon a painted ocean.

And the Albatross begins to be avenged.

Water, water, every where,
And all the boards did shrink;
Water, water, every where,
Nor any drop to drink.

The very deep did rot: O Christ!
That ever this should be!
Yea, slimy things did crawl with
    legs
Upon the slimy sea.

A spirit had followed them; one of the invisible inhabitants of this planet, neither departed souls nor angels; concerning whom the Jew Josephus, and the Platonic Constantionpolitan Michael Psellus, may be consulted. They are very numerous, and there is no climate or element without one or more.

About, about, in reel and rout
The death-fires danced at night;
The water, like a witch's oils,
Burnt green, and blue and white.

And some in dreams assurèd were
Of the Spirit that plagued us so;
Nine fathom deep he had
    followed us
From the land of mist and snow.

And every tongue, through utter
    drought,
Was withered at the root;
We could not speak, no more
    than if
We had been choked with soot.

The shipmates, in their sore distress, would fain throw the whole guilt on the ancient Mariner: in sign whereof they hang the dead sea-bird round his neck.

Ah! well a-day! what evil looks
Had I from old and young!
Instead of the cross, the
    Albatross
About my neck was hung.

Mine enemy is growing old

Emily Dickinson

Mine enemy is growing old,—
I have at last revenge.
The palate of the hate departs;
If any would avenge,—

Let him be quick, the viand flits,
It is a faded meat.
Anger as soon as fed is dead;
'T is starving makes it fat.

Appeal
E. Nesbit

Daphnis dearest, wherefore weave me
Webs of lies lest truth should grieve me?
I could pardon much, believe me:
Dower me, Daphnis, or bereave me,
Kill me, kill me, love me, leave me—
Damn me, dear, but don't deceive me!

Revenge

Letitia Elizabeth Landon

Ay, gaze upon her rose-wreathed hair,
   And gaze upon her smile;
Seem as you drank the very air
   Her breath perfumed the while;

And wake for her the gifted line,
   That wild and witching lay,
And swear your heart is as a shrine,
   That only owns her sway.

'Tis well: I am revenged at last,—
   Mark you that scornful cheek,—
The eye averted as you pass'd,
   Spoke more than words could speak.

Ay, now by all the bitter tears
   That I have shed for thee,—
The racking doubts, the burning fears,—
   Avenged they well may be—

By the nights pass'd in sleepless care,
   The days of endless woe;
All that you taught my heart to bear,
   All that yourself will know.

I would not wish to see you laid
   Within an early tomb;
I should forget how you betray'd,
   And only weep your doom:

But this is fitting punishment,
   To live and love in vain,—
Oh my wrung heart, be thou content,
   And feed upon his pain.

Go thou and watch her lightest sigh,—
   Thine own it will not be;
And bask beneath her sunny eye,—
   It will not turn on thee.

'Tis well: the rack, the chain, the wheel,
   Far better hadst thou proved;
Ev'n I could almost pity feel,
   For thou art not beloved.

Fletcher McGee

Edgar Lee Masters

She took my strength by minutes,
She took my life by hours,
She drained me like a fevered moon
That saps the spinning world.
The days went by like shadows,
The minutes wheeled like stars.
She took the pity from my heart,
And made it into smiles.
She was a hunk of sculptor's clay,
My secret thoughts were fingers
They flew behind her pensive brow
And lined it deep with pain.
They set the lips, and sagged the cheeks,
And drooped the eyes with sorrow.
My soul had entered in the clay,
Fighting like seven devils.
It was not mine, it was not hers;
She held it, but its struggles
Modeled a face she hated,
And a face I feared to see.
I beat the windows, shook the bolts.
I hid me in a corner—
And then she died and haunted me,
And hunted me for life.

To Sophronia

Hannah Griffitts

I've neither Reserve or aversion to Man,
(I assure you Sophronia in jingle)
But to keep my dear Liberty, long as I can,
Is the Reason I chuse to live single,
My Sense, or the Want of it—free you may jest
And censure, dispise, or impeach,
But the Happiness center'd within my own Breast,
Is luckily out of your reach.
The Men, (as a Friend) I prefer, I esteem,
And love them as well as I ought
But to fix all my Happiness, solely in Him
Was never my Wish or my Thought,
The cowardly Nymph, you so often reprove,
Is not frighted by Giants like these,
Leave me to enjoy the sweet Freedom I love
And go marry—as soon as you please.

"All Heaven in a Rage"
William Blake

From **AUGURIES OF INNOCENCE**

To see a World in a Grain of Sand
And a Heaven in a Wild Flower
Hold Infinity in the palm of your hand
And Eternity in an hour

A Robin Red breast in a Cage
Puts all Heaven in a Rage
A Dove house filld with Doves & Pigeons
Shudders Hell thr' all its regions
A dog starvd at his Masters Gate
Predicts the ruin of the State
A Horse misusd upon the Road
Calls to Heaven for Human blood
Each outcry of the hunted Hare
A fibre from the Brain does tear
A Skylark wounded in the wing
A Cherubim does cease to sing
The Game Cock clipd & armd for fight
Does the Rising Sun affright
Every Wolfs & Lions howl
Raises from Hell a Human Soul
The wild deer, wandring here & there
Keeps the Human Soul from Care

The Lamb misusd breeds Public Strife
And yet forgives the Butchers knife
The Bat that flits at close of Eve
Has left the Brain that wont Believe
The Owl that calls upon the Night
Speaks the Unbelievers fright
He who shall hurt the little Wren
Shall never be belovd by Men
He who the Ox to wrath has movd
Shall never be by Woman lovd
The wanton Boy that kills the Fly
Shall feel the Spiders enmity

I Know My Soul

Claude McKay

I plucked my soul out of its secret place,
And held it to the mirror of my eye,
To see it like a star against the sky,
A twitching body quivering in space,
A spark of passion shining on my face.
And I explored it to determine why
This awful key to my infinity
Conspires to rob me of sweet joy and grace.
And if the sign may not be fully read,
If I can comprehend but not control,
I need not gloom my days with futile dread,
Because I see a part and not the whole.
Contemplating the strange, I'm comforted
By this narcotic thought: I know my soul.

A Voice From The Dungeon

Anne Brontë

I'm buried now; I've done with life;
I've done with hate, revenge and strife;
I've done with joy, and hope and love
And all the bustling world above.

Long have I dwelt forgotten here
In pining woe and dull despair;
This place of solitude and gloom
Must be my dungeon and my tomb.

No hope, no pleasure can I find:
I am grown weary of my mind;
Often in balmy sleep I try
To gain a rest from misery,

And in one hour of calm repose
To find a respite from my woes,
But dreamless sleep is not for me
And I am still in misery.

I dream of liberty, 'tis true,
But then I dream of sorrow too,
Of blood and guilt and horrid woes,
Of tortured friends and happy foes;

I dream about the world, but then
I dream of fiends instead of men;
Each smiling hope so quickly fades
And such a lurid gloom pervades

That world—that when I wake and see
Those dreary phantoms fade and flee,
Even in my dungeon I can smile,
And taste of joy a little while.

And yet it is not always so;
I dreamt a little while ago
That all was as it used to be:
A fresh free wind passed over me;

It was a pleasant summer's day,
The sun shone forth with cheering ray,
Methought a little lovely child
Looked up into my face and smiled.

My heart was full, I wept for joy,
It was my own, my darling boy;
I clasped him to my breast and he
Kissed me and laughed in childish glee.

Just then I heard in whisper sweet
A well known voice my name repeat.
His father stood before my eyes;
I gazed at him in mute surprise,

I thought he smiled and spoke to me,
But still in silent ecstasy
I gazed at him; I could not speak;
I uttered one long piercing shriek.

Alas! Alas! That cursed scream
Aroused me from my heavenly dream;
I looked around in wild despair,
I called them, but they were not there;
The father and the child are gone,
And I must live and die alone.

The Apparition

John Donne

When by thy scorn, O murderess, I am dead,
   And that thou think'st thee free
From all solicitation from me,
Then shall my ghost come to thy bed,
And thee, feigned vestal, in worse arms shall see;
Then thy sick taper will begin to wink,
And he, whose thou art then, being tired before,
Will, if thou stir, or pinch to wake him, think
   Thou call'st for more,
And in false sleep will from thee shrink,
And then, poor aspen wretch, neglected thou
Bathed in a cold quicksilver sweat wilt lie
   A verier ghost than I;
What I will say, I will not tell thee now,
Lest that preserve thee; and since my love is spent,
I had rather thou shouldst painfully repent,
Than by my threatenings rest still innocent.

Invictus

William Ernest Henley

Out of the night that covers me,
　Black as the pit from pole to pole.
I thank whatever gods may be
　For my unconquerable soul.

In the fell clutch of circumstance
　I have not winced nor cried aloud.
Under the bludgeonings of chance
　My head is bloody, but unbowed.

Beyond this place of wrath and tears
　Looms but the Horror of the shade,
And yet the menace of the years
　Finds, and shall find me, unafraid.

It matters not how strait the gate,
　How charged with punishments the scroll,
I am the master of my fate:
　I am the captain of my soul.

Forgive and Forget

Jean Blewett

I'll tell you the sweetest thing, dear heart,
   I'll tell you the sweetest thing—
'Tis saying to one that we love: "Forgive
   The careless words and the sting;
Forgive and forget, and be friends once more,
   For the world is an empty place
Without the light of your warm, true eyes,
   And the smile of your tender face."

O the kissing and making up again,
   And the tender whispering!
I'll tell you the sweetest thing, dear heart,
   I'll tell you the sweetest thing.

I'll tell you the saddest thing, dear heart,
   I'll tell you the saddest thing:
'Tis coming to one that we love full well,
   Some tender message to bring.

And loitering, loitering, by the way—
   Held back by a foolish pride—
Till it's all too late to say "Forgive!"
   When at length we reach her side.

For the ears are heavy and cannot hear,
    And the chill lips cannot move
To whisper "Peace," though our hearts may break
    With longing, and pain, and love,

O this coming too late with our tenderness!
    O the passionate tears that spring!
I'll tell you the saddest thing, dear heart,
    I'll tell you the saddest thing!

Then let us make haste to be friends again,
    Make haste to fold to our breast
The one we have hurt by word and deed,
    Though we loved that one the best.
"Forgive and forget! Forgive and forget!"
    O warm in the tear-wet eyes
Is the glow and the gleam of a golden light
    From the shores of Paradise.

O the kissing and making up again,
    And the tender whispering!
I'll tell you the sweetest thing, dear heart,
    I'll tell you the sweetest thing.

"Th' infernal Serpent"

John Milton

From **PARADISE LOST, BOOK I**

Satan, in the shape of a serpent, and driven by envy
and a desire for revenge against God for having him
cast out of Heaven, decides to deceive Eve, causing
the Fall of Man.

Th' infernal Serpent; he it was whose guile,
Stirred up with envy and revenge, deceived
The mother of mankind, what time his pride
Had cast him out from Heaven, with all his host
Of rebel Angels, by whose aid, aspiring
To set himself in glory above his peers,
He trusted to have equalled the Most High,
If he opposed, and with ambitious aim
Against the throne and monarchy of God,
Raised impious war in Heaven and battle proud,
With vain attempt. Him the Almighty Power
Hurled headlong flaming from th' ethereal sky,
With hideous ruin and combustion, down
To bottomless perdition, there to dwell
In adamantine chains and penal fire,
Who durst defy th' Omnipotent to arms.

Nine times the space that measures day
   and night
To mortal men, he, with his horrid crew,
Lay vanquished, rolling in the fiery gulf,
Confounded, though immortal. But his doom
Reserved him to more wrath; for now the thought
Both of lost happiness and lasting pain
Torments him: round he throws his baleful eyes,
That witnessed huge affliction and dismay,
Mixed with obdurate pride and steadfast hate.
At once, as far as Angels ken, he views
The dismal situation waste and wild.
A dungeon horrible, on all sides round,
As one great furnace flamed; yet from those flames
No light; but rather darkness visible
Served only to discover sights of woe,
Regions of sorrow, doleful shades, where peace
And rest can never dwell, hope never comes
That comes to all, but torture without end
Still urges, and a fiery deluge, fed
With ever-burning sulphur unconsumed.

Folklore

/FOHK-*lor*/ – noun

The traditional, often unwritten, stories and beliefs that are shared among a community of people and told over many generations.

"Tales, marvellous tales"

James Elroy Flecker

From the prologue of **THE GOLDEN JOURNEY TO
SAMARKAND**

We who with songs beguile your pilgrimage
    And swear that Beauty lives though lilies die,
We Poets of the proud old lineage
    Who sing to find your hearts, we know not why,—

What shall we tell you? Tales, marvellous tales
    Of ships and stars and isles where good men rest,
Where nevermore the rose of sunset pales,
    And winds and shadows fall towards the West:

And there the world's first huge white-bearded kings
    In dim glades sleeping, murmur in their sleep,
And closer round their breasts the ivý clings,
    Cutting its pathway slow and red and deep.

Ode
Arthur O'Shaughnessy

Extract

We are the music makers,
    And we are the dreamers of dreams,
Wandering by lone sea-breakers,
    And sitting by desolate streams;—
World-losers and world-forsakers,
    On whom the pale moon gleams:
Yet we are the movers and shakers
    Of the world for ever, it seems.

Fairy Song
Louisa May Alcott

The moonlight fades from flower and tree,
    And the stars dim one by one;
The tale is told, the song is sung,
    And the Fairy feast is done.
The night-wind rocks the sleeping flowers,
    And sings to them, soft and low.
The early birds erelong will wake:
    'Tis time for the Elves to go.

O'er the sleeping earth we silently pass,
    Unseen by mortal eye,
And send sweet dreams, as we lightly float
    Through the quiet moonlit sky;—
For the stars' soft eyes alone may see,
    And the flowers alone may know,
The feasts we hold, the tales we tell:
    So 'tis time for the Elves to go.

From bird, and blossom, and bee,
    We learn the lessons they teach;
And seek, by kindly deeds, to win
    A loving friend in each.
And though unseen on earth we dwell,
    Sweet voices whisper low,
And gentle hearts most joyously greet
    The Elves where'er they go.

When next we meet in the Fairy dell,
    May the silver moon's soft light
Shine then on faces gay as now,
    And Elfin hearts as light.
Now spread each wing, for the eastern sky
    With sunlight soon will glow.
The morning star shall light us home:
    Farewell! for the Elves must go.

A Boat, Beneath a Sunny Sky
Lewis Carroll

A boat, beneath a sunny sky
Lingering onward dreamily
In an evening of July—

Children three that nestle near,
Eager eye and willing ear,
Pleased a simple tale to hear—

Long has paled that sunny sky;
Echoes fade and memories die;
Autumn frosts have slain July.

Still she haunts me, phantomwise
Alice moving under skies
Never seen by waking eyes.

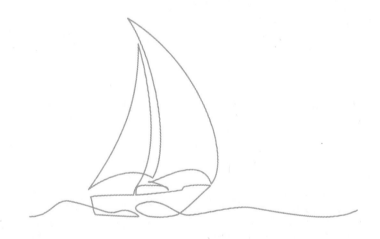

Children yet, the tale to hear,
Eager eye and willing ear,
Lovingly shall nestle near.

In a Wonderland they lie,
Dreaming as the days go by,
Dreaming as the summers die;

Ever drifting down the stream—
Lingering in the golden gleam—
Life, what is it but a dream?

The Apparition

Herman Melville

(A Retrospect)

Convulsions came; and, where the field
    Long slept in pastoral green,
A goblin-mountain was upheaved
(Sure the scared sense was all deceived),
    Marl-glen and slag-ravine.

The unreserve of Ill was there,
    The clinkers in her last retreat;
But, ere the eye could take it in,
Or mind could comprehension win,
    It sunk!—and at our feet.

So, then, Solidity's a crust—
    The core of fire below;
All may go well for many a year,
But who can think without a fear
    Of horrors that happen so?

The Sound of the Sea
Henry Wadsworth Longfellow

The sea awoke at midnight from its sleep,
    And round the pebbly beaches far and wide
    I heard the first wave of the rising tide
    Rush onward with uninterrupted sweep;
A voice out of the silence of the deep,
    A sound mysteriously multiplied
    As of a cataract from the mountain's side,
    Or roar of winds upon a wooded steep.
So comes to us at times, from the unknown
    And inaccessible solitudes of being,
    The rushing of the sea-tides of the soul;
And inspirations, that we deem our own,
    Are some divine foreshadowing and foreseeing
    Of things beyond our reason or control.

A London Thoroughfare.
2 A.M.

Amy Lowell

They have watered the street,
It shines in the glare of lamps,
Cold, white lamps,
And lies
Like a slow-moving river,
Barred with silver and black.
Cabs go down it,
One,
And then another.
Between them I hear the shuffling of feet.
Tramps doze on the window-ledges,
Night-walkers pass along the sidewalks.
The city is squalid and sinister,
With the silver-barred street in the midst,
Slow-moving,
A river leading nowhere.

Opposite my window,
The moon cuts,
Clear and round,
Through the plum-coloured night.
She cannot light the city:
It is too bright.
It has white lamps,
And glitters coldly.

I stand in the window and watch the moon.
She is thin and lustreless,
But I love her.
I know the moon,
And this is an alien city.

"My love of Freedom"

Phillis Wheatley

Extract from **To the Right Honourable William, Earl of Dartmouth**

Should you, my lord, while you peruse my song,
Wonder from whence my love of Freedom sprung,
Whence flow these wishes for the common good,
By feeling hearts alone best understood,
I, young in life, by seeming cruel fate
Was snatch'd from Afric's fancy'd happy seat:
What pangs excruciating must molest,
What sorrows labour in my parent's breast?
Steel'd was that soul and by no misery mov'd
That from a father seiz'd his babe belov'd:
Such, such my case. And can I then but pray
Others may never feel tyrannic sway?

Speak of the North! A Lonely Moor

Charlotte Brontë

Speak of the North! A lonely moor
Silent and dark and tractless swells,
The waves of some wild streamlet pour
Hurriedly through its ferny dells.

Profoundly still the twilight air,
Lifeless the landscape; so we deem
Till like a phantom gliding near
A stag bends down to drink the stream.

And far away a mountain zone,
A cold, white waste of snow-drifts lies,
And one star, large and soft and lone,
Silently lights the unclouded skies.

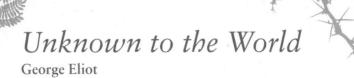

Unknown to the World

George Eliot

Extract adapted from the novel **FELIX HOLT, THE RADICAL**

The poets have told us
of a dolorous enchanted forest
in the under world.

The thorn-bushes there,
and the thick-barked stems,
have human histories hidden in them;

the power of unuttered cries
dwells in the passionless-seeming branches,

and the red warm blood is darkly feeding
the quivering nerves of a sleepless memory
that watches through all dreams.

These things are a parable.

Alone

Edgar Allan Poe

From childhood's hour I have not been
As others were—I have not seen
As others saw—I could not bring
My passions from a common spring—
From the same source I have not taken
My sorrow—I could not awaken
My heart to joy at the same tone—
And all I lov'd—*I* lov'd alone—
Then—in my childhood—in the dawn
Of a most stormy life—was drawn
From ev'ry depth of good and ill
The mystery which binds me still—
From the torrent, or the fountain—
From the red cliff of the mountain—
From the sun that 'round me roll'd
In its autumn tint of gold—
From the lightning in the sky
As it pass'd me flying by—
From the thunder, and the storm—
And the cloud that took the form
(When the rest of Heaven was blue)
Of a demon in my view—

The Stolen Child

W. B. Yeats

Where dips the rocky highland
Of Sleuth Wood in the lake,
There lies a leafy island
Where flapping herons wake
The drowsy water-rats;
There we've hid our faery vats,
Full of berries
And of reddest stolen cherries.
Come away, O human child!
To the waters and the wild
With a faery, hand in hand,
For the world's more full of weeping than you can
    understand.

Where the wave of moonlight glosses
The dim grey sands with light,
Far off by furthest Rosses
We foot it all the night,
Weaving olden dances,
Mingling hands and mingling glances
Till the moon has taken flight;
To and fro we leap
And chase the frothy bubbles,
While the world is full of troubles
And anxious in its sleep.
Come away, O human child!
To the waters and the wild
With a faery, hand in hand,

*For the world's more full of weeping than you can
    understand.*

Where the wandering water gushes
From the hills above Glen-Car,
In pools among the rushes
That scarce could bathe a star,
We seek for slumbering trout
And whispering in their ears
Give them unquiet dreams;
Leaning softly out
From ferns that drop their tears
Over the young streams.
Come away, O human child!
To the waters and the wild
With a faery, hand in hand,
*For the world's more full of weeping than you can
    understand.*

Away with us he's going,
The solemn-eyed:
He'll hear no more the lowing
Of the calves on the warm hillside
Or the kettle on the hob
Sing peace into his breast,
Or see the brown mice bob
Round and round the oatmeal-chest.
For he comes, the human child,
To the waters and the wild
With a faery, hand in hand,
*For the world's more full of weeping than he can
    understand.*

City Dusk

F. Scott Fitzgerald

Come out.... out
To this inevitable night of mine
Oh you drinker of new wine,
Here's pageantry.... Here's carnival,
Rich dusk, dim streets and all
The whispering of city night....

I have closed my book of fading harmonies,
(The shadows fell across me in the park)
And my soul was sad with violins and trees,
And I was sick for dark,
When suddenly it hastened by me, bringing
Thousands of lights, a haunting breeze,
And a night of streets and singing....

I shall know you by your eager feet
And by your pale, pale hair;
I'll whisper happy incoherent things
While I'm waiting for you there....

All the faces unforgettable in dusk
Will blend to yours,
And the footsteps like a thousand overtures
Will blend to yours,
And there will be more drunkenness than wine
In the softness of your eyes on mine....

Faint violins where lovely ladies dine,
The brushing of skirts, the voices of the night
And all the lure of friendly eyes.... Ah there
We'll drift like summer sounds upon the summer air....

The Ivy Green

Charles Dickens

Oh, a dainty plant is the Ivy green,
That creepeth o'er ruins old!
Of right choice food are his meals, I ween,
In his cell so lone and cold.
The wall must be crumbled, the stone decayed,
To pleasure his dainty whim:
And the mouldering dust that years have made,
Is a merry meal for him.
      Creeping where no life is seen,
      A rare old plant is the Ivy green.

Fast he stealeth on, though he wears no wings,
And a staunch old heart has he.
How closely he twineth, how tight he clings,
To his friend the huge Oak Tree!
And slily he traileth along the ground,
And his leaves he gently waves,
As he joyously hugs and crawleth round
The rich mould of dead men's graves.
      Creeping where grim death has been,
      A rare old plant is the Ivy green.

Whole ages have fled and their works decayed,
And nations have scattered been;
But the stout old Ivy shall never fade,
From its hale and hearty green.
The brave old plant in its lonely days,
Shall fatten upon the past:
For the stateliest building man can raise,
Is the Ivy's food at last.

      Creeping on, where time has been,
      A rare old plant is the Ivy green.

"Boat Stealing"

William Wordsworth

From **THE PRELUDE, Book 1 (1850 version)**

One summer evening (led by her) I found
A little boat tied to a willow tree
Within a rocky cave, its usual home.
Straight I unloosed her chain, and stepping in
Pushed from the shore. It was an act of stealth
And troubled pleasure, nor without the voice
Of mountain-echoes did my boat move on;
Leaving behind her still, on either side,
Small circles glittering idly in the moon,
Until they melted all into one track
Of sparkling light. But now, like one who rows,
Proud of his skill, to reach a chosen point
With an unswerving line, I fixed my view
Upon the summit of a craggy ridge,
The horizon's utmost boundary; far above
Was nothing but the stars and the grey sky.
She was an elfin pinnace; lustily
I dipped my oars into the silent lake,
And, as I rose upon the stroke, my boat
Went heaving through the water like a swan;

When, from behind that craggy steep till then
The horizon's bound, a huge peak, black and huge,
As if with voluntary power instinct
Upreared its head. I struck and struck again,
And growing still in stature the grim shape
Towered up between me and the stars, and still,
For so it seemed, with purpose of its own
And measured motion like a living thing,
Strode after me. With trembling oars I turned,
And through the silent water stole my way
Back to the covert of the willow tree;
There in her mooring-place I left my bark,—
And through the meadows homeward went, in grave
And serious mood; but after I had seen
That spectacle, for many days, my brain
Worked with a dim and undetermined sense
Of unknown modes of being; o'er my thoughts
There hung a darkness, call it solitude
Or blank desertion. No familiar shapes
Remained, no pleasant images of trees,
Of sea or sky, no colours of green fields;
But huge and mighty forms, that do not live
Like living men, moved slowly through the mind
By day, and were a trouble to my dreams.

The Weary Blues

Langston Hughes

Droning a drowsy syncopated tune,
Rocking back and forth to a mellow croon,
    I heard a Negro play.
Down on Lenox Avenue the other night
By the pale dull pallor of an old gas light
    He did a lazy sway....
    He did a lazy sway....
To the tune o' those Weary Blues.
With his ebony hands on each ivory key
He made that poor piano moan with melody.
    O Blues!
Swaying to and fro on his rickety stool
He played that sad raggy tune like a musical fool.
    Sweet Blues!

Coming from a black man's soul.
    O Blues!
In a deep song voice with a melancholy tone
I heard that Negro sing, that old piano moan—
    "Ain't got nobody in all this world,
        Ain't got nobody but ma self.
        I's gwine to quit ma frownin'
        And put ma troubles on the shelf."

Thump, thump, thump, went his foot on the floor.
He played a few chords then he sang some more—
    "I got the Weary Blues
        And I can't be satisfied.
        Got the Weary Blues
        And can't be satisfied—
        I ain't happy no mo'
        And I wish that I had died."
And far into the night he crooned that tune.
The stars went out and so did the moon.
The singer stopped playing and went to bed
While the Weary Blues echoed through his head.
He slept like a rock or a man that's dead.

Stopping by Woods on a Snowy Evening

Robert Frost

Whose woods these are I think I know.
His house is in the village though;
He will not see me stopping here
To watch his woods fill up with snow.

My little horse must think it queer
To stop without a farmhouse near
Between the woods and frozen lake
The darkest evening of the year.

He gives his harness bells a shake
To ask if there is some mistake.
The only other sound's the sweep
Of easy wind and downy flake.

The woods are lovely, dark and deep,
But I have promises to keep,
And miles to go before I sleep,
And miles to go before I sleep.

Saturday Market

Charlotte Mew

Bury your heart in some deep green hollow
   Or hide it up in a kind old tree;
Better still, give it the swallow
   When she goes over the sea.

In Saturday Market there's eggs a 'plenty
   And dead-alive ducks with their legs tied down,
Grey old gaffers and boys of twenty—
   Girls and the women of the town—
Pitchers and sugar-sticks, ribbons and laces,
   Posies and whips and dicky-birds' seed,
Silver pieces and smiling faces,
   In Saturday Market they've all they need.

What were you showing in Saturday Market
   That set it grinning from end to end
Girls and gaffers and boys of twenty—?
   Cover it close with your shawl, my friend—
Hasten you home with the laugh behind you,
   Over the down—, out of sight,
Fasten your door, though no one will find you
   No one will look on a Market night.

See, you, the shawl is wet, take out from under
  The red dead thing—. In the white of the moon
On the flags does it stir again? Well, and no wonder!
  Best make an end of it; bury it soon.
If there is blood on the hearth who'll know it?
  Or blood on the stairs,
When a murder is over and done why show it?
  In Saturday Market nobody cares.

Then lie you straight on your bed for a short, short
      weeping
  And still, for a long, long rest,
There's never a one in the town so sure of sleeping
  As you, in the house on the down with a hole in
      your breast.

      Think no more of the swallow,
        Forget, you, the sea,
  Never again remember the deep green hollow
        Or the top of the kind old tree!

Dawn in New York
Claude McKay

The Dawn! The Dawn! The crimson-tinted, comes
Out of the low still skies, over the hills,
Manhattan's roofs and spires and cheerless domes!
The Dawn! My spirit to its spirit thrills.
Almost the mighty city is asleep,
No pushing crowd, no tramping, tramping feet.
But here and there a few cars groaning creep
Along, above, and underneath the street,
Bearing their strangely-ghostly burdens by,
The women and the men of garish nights,
Their eyes wine-weakened and their clothes awry,
Grotesques beneath the strong electric lights.
The shadows wane. The Dawn comes to New York.
And I go darkly-rebel to my work.

Beauty
Sappho

Translated by Dante Gabriel Rossetti (1828–1882)

I

Like the sweet apple which reddens upon the topmost
  bough,

A-top on the top-most twig,—which the pluckers forgot,
  somehow,—

Forget it not, nay; but got it not, for none could get it till
  now.

II

Like the wild hyacinth flower which on the hills is found,

Which the passing feet of the shepherds for ever tear and
  wound,

Until the purple blossom is trodden into the ground.

The Ballad of Camden Town

James Elroy Flecker

I walked with Maisie long years back
    The streets of Camden Town,
I splendid in my suit of black,
    And she divine in brown.

Hers was a proud and noble face,
    A secret heart, and eyes
Like water in a lonely place
    Beneath unclouded skies.

A bed, a chest, a faded mat,
    And broken chairs a few,
Were all we had to grace our flat
    In Hazel Avenue.

But I could walk to Hampstead Heath,
    And crown her head with daisies,
And watch the streaming world beneath,
    And men with other Maisies.

When I was ill and she was pale
    And empty stood our store,
She left the latchkey on its nail,
    And saw me nevermore.

Perhaps she cast herself away
    Lest both of us should drown:
Perhaps she feared to die, as they
    Who die in Camden Town.

What came of her? The bitter nights
    Destroy the rose and lily,
And souls are lost among the lights
    Of painted Piccadilly.

What came of her? The river flows
    So deep and wide and stilly,
And waits to catch the fallen rose
    And clasp the broken lily.

I dream she dwells in London still
    And breathes the evening air,
And often walk to Primrose Hill,
    And hope to meet her there.

Once more together we will live,
    For I will find her yet:
I have so little to forgive;
    So much, I can't forget.

The Raven

Edgar Allan Poe

Once upon a midnight dreary, while I pondered, weak
   and weary,
Over many a quaint and curious volume of forgotten
   lore—
While I nodded, nearly napping, suddenly there came a
   tapping,
As of some one gently rapping, rapping at my chamber
   door.
"'Tis some visiter," I muttered, "tapping at my
   chamber door—
                        Only this and nothing more."

Ah, distinctly I remember it was in the bleak
   December;
And each separate dying ember wrought its ghost upon
   the floor.
Eagerly I wished the morrow;—vainly I had sought to
   borrow
From my books surcease of sorrow—sorrow for the
   lost Lenore—
For the rare and radiant maiden whom the angels
   name Lenore—
                        Nameless *here* for evermore.

And the silken, sad, uncertain rustling of each purple
  curtain
Thrilled me—filled me with fantastic terrors never felt
  before;
So that now, to still the beating of my heart, I stood
  repeating
"'Tis some visiter entreating entrance at my chamber
  door—
Some late visiter entreating entrance at my chamber
  door;—
                    This it is and nothing more."

Presently my soul grew stronger; hesitating then no
  longer,
"Sir," said I, "or Madam, truly your forgiveness I
  implore;
But the fact is I was napping, and so gently you came
  rapping,
And so faintly you came tapping, tapping at my
  chamber door,
That I scarce was sure I heard you"—here I opened
  wide the door;—
                    Darkness there and nothing more.

Deep into that darkness peering, long I stood there
  wondering, fearing,
Doubting, dreaming dreams no mortal ever dared to
  dream before;
But the silence was unbroken, and the stillness gave no
  token,

143

And the only word there spoken was the whispered
    word, "Lenore?"
This I whispered, and an echo murmured back the
    word, "Lenore!"—

               Merely this and nothing more.

Back into the chamber turning, all my soul within me
    burning,
Soon again I heard a tapping somewhat louder than
    before.
"Surely," said I, "surely that is something at my
    window lattice;
Let me see, then, what thereat is, and this mystery
    explore—
Let my heart be still a moment and this mystery
    explore;—

            'Tis the wind and nothing more!"

Open here I flung the shutter, when, with many a flirt
    and flutter,
In there stepped a stately Raven of the saintly days of
    yore;
Not the least obeisance made he; not a minute stopped
    or stayed he;
But, with mien of lord or lady, perched above my
    chamber door—
Perched upon a bust of Pallas just above my chamber
    door—

          Perched, and sat, and nothing more.

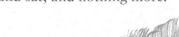

Then this ebony bird beguiling my sad fancy into
    smiling,
By the grave and stern decorum of the countenance it
    wore,
"Though thy crest be shorn and shaven, thou," I said,
    "art sure no craven,
Ghastly grim and ancient Raven wandering from the
    Nightly shore—
Tell me what thy lordly name is on the Night's
    Plutonian shore!"
                    Quoth the Raven "Nevermore."

Much I marvelled this ungainly fowl to hear discourse
    so plainly,
Though its answer little meaning—little relevancy
    bore;
For we cannot help agreeing that no living human
    being
Ever yet was blessed with seeing bird above his
    chamber door—
Bird or beast upon the sculptured bust above his
    chamber door,
                    With such name as "Nevermore."

But the Raven, sitting lonely on the placid bust, spoke
    only
That one word, as if his soul in that one word he did
    outpour.

Nothing farther then he uttered—not a feather then he
    fluttered—
Till I scarcely more than muttered "Other friends have
    flown before—
On the morrow *he* will leave me, as my Hopes have
    flown before."
                        Then the bird said "Nevermore."

Startled at the stillness broken by reply so aptly
    spoken,
"Doubtless," said I, "what it utters is its only stock
    and store
Caught from some unhappy master whom unmerciful
    Disaster
Followed fast and followed faster till his songs one
    burden bore—
Till the dirges of his Hope that melancholy burden
    bore
                        Of 'Never—nevermore'."

But the Raven still beguiling my sad fancy into smiling,
Straight I wheeled a cushioned seat in front of bird,
    and bust and door;
Then, upon the velvet sinking, I betook myself to
    linking
Fancy unto fancy, thinking what this ominous bird of
    yore—
What this grim, ungainly, ghastly, gaunt, and ominous
    bird of yore
                        Meant in croaking "Nevermore."

This I sat engaged in guessing, but no syllable
    expressing
To the fowl whose fiery eyes now burned into my
    bosom's core;
This and more I sat divining, with my head at ease
    reclining
On the cushion's velvet lining that the lamp-light
    gloated o'er,
But whose velvet-violet lining with the lamp-light
    gloating o'er,
                    She shall press, ah, nevermore!

Then, methought, the air grew denser, perfumed from
    an unseen censer
Swung by seraphim whose foot-falls tinkled on the
    tufted floor.
"Wretch," I cried, "thy God hath lent thee—by these
    angels he hath sent thee
Respite—respite and nepenthe from thy memories of
    Lenore;
Quaff, oh quaff this kind nepenthe and forget this lost
    Lenore!"
                    Quoth the Raven "Nevermore."

"Prophet!" said I, "thing of evil—prophet still, if bird
    or devil—
Whether Tempter sent, or whether tempest tossed thee
    here ashore,
Desolate yet all undaunted, on this desert land
    enchanted—

On this home by Horror haunted—tell me truly, I
    implore—
Is there—*is* there balm in Gilead—tell me—tell me, I
    implore!"
                    Quoth the Raven "Nevermore."

"Prophet!" said I, "thing of evil—prophet still, if bird
    or devil!
By that Heaven that bends above us—by that God we
    both adore—
Tell this soul with sorrow laden if, within the distant
    Aidenn,
It shall clasp a sainted maiden whom the angels name
    Lenore—
Clasp a rare and radiant maiden whom the angels
    name Lenore."
                    Quoth the Raven "Nevermore."

"Be that word our sign of parting, bird or fiend!" I
    shrieked, upstarting—
"Get thee back into the tempest and the Night's
    Plutonian shore!
Leave no black plume as a token of that lie thy soul
    hath spoken!
Leave my loneliness unbroken—quit the bust above my
    door!
Take thy beak from out my heart, and take thy form
    from off my door!"
                    Quoth the Raven "Nevermore."

And the Raven, never flitting, still is sitting, *still* is
    sitting
On the pallid bust of Pallas just above my chamber
    door;
And his eyes have all the seeming of a demon's that is
    dreaming,
And the lamp-light o'er him streaming throws his
    shadow on the floor;
And my soul from out that shadow that lies floating on
    the floor
                                  Shall be lifted—nevermore!

Peace

/*peess*/ – noun

After anxiety, distress, and great war comes a
state of harmony, friendliness, and quiet. Like
seeing daylight after a long night.

Peace

Sara Teasdale

Peace flows into me
   As the tide to the pool by the shore;
   It is mine forevermore,
It ebbs not back like the sea.

I am the pool of blue
   That worships the vivid sky;
   My hopes were heaven-high,
They are all fulfilled in you.

I am the pool of gold
   When sunset burns and dies,—
   You are my deepening skies,
Give me your stars to hold.

Let us go, then, exploring

Virginia Woolf

Let us go, then, exploring
This summer morning,
When all are adoring
The plum-blossom and the bee.
And humming and hawing
Let us ask of the starling
What he may think
On the brink
Of the dust-bin whence he picks
Among the sticks
Combings of scullion's hair.
What's life, we ask;
Life, Life, Life! cries the bird
As if he had heard....

Deep in the Quiet Wood

James Weldon Johnson

Are you bowed down in heart?
Do you but hear the clashing discords and the din
    of life?
Then come away, come to the peaceful wood.
Here bathe your soul in silence. Listen! Now,
From out the palpitating solitude
Do you not catch, yet faint, elusive strains?
They are above, around, within you, everywhere.
Silently listen! Clear, and still more clear, they come.
They bubble up in rippling notes, and swell in
    singing tones.
Now let your soul run the whole gamut of the
    wondrous scale
Until, responsive to the tonic chord,
It touches the diapason of God's grand
    cathedral organ,
Filling earth for you with heavenly peace
And holy harmonies.

I many times thought Peace had come

Emily Dickinson

I many times thought peace had come,
When peace was far away;
As wrecked men deem they sight the land
At centre of the sea,

And struggle slacker, but to prove,
As hopelessly as I,
How many the fictitious shores
Before the harbor lie.

The Little Waves of Breffny

Eva Gore-Booth

The grand road from the mountain goes shining to
   the sea,
And there is traffic in it and many a horse and cart,
But the little roads of Cloonagh are dearer far to me,
And the little roads of Cloonagh go rambling
   through my heart.

A great storm from the ocean goes shouting o'er
   the hill,
And there is glory in it and terror on the wind,
But the haunted air of twilight is very strange and still,
And the little winds of twilight are dearer to my mind.

The great waves of the Atlantic sweep storming on
   their way,
Shining green and silver with the hidden herring shoal,
But the Little Waves of Breffny have drenched my heart
   in spray,
And the Little Waves of Breffny go stumbling through
   my soul.

The Sparrow

Paul Laurence Dunbar

A little bird, with plumage brown,
Beside my window flutters down,
A moment chirps its little strain,
Ten taps upon my window-pane,
And chirps again, and hops along,
To call my notice to its song;
But I work on, nor heed its lay,
Till, in neglect, it flies away.

So birds of peace and hope and love
Come fluttering earthward from above,
To settle on life's window-sills,
And ease our load of earthly ills;
But we, in traffic's rush and din
Too deep engaged to let them in,
With deadened heart and sense plod on,
Nor know our loss till they are gone.

Comrades

Ella Wheeler Wilcox

I and my Soul are alone to-day,
    All in the shining weather;
We were sick of the world, and we put it away,
    So we could rejoice together.

Our host, the Sun, in the blue, blue sky,
    Is mixing a rare, sweet wine,
In the burnished gold of his cup on high,
    For me, and this Soul of mine.

We find it a safe and a royal drink,
    And a cure from every pain:
It helps us to love, and helps us to think,
    And strengthens body and brain.

And sitting here, with my Soul alone,
    Where the yellow sun-rays fall,
Of all the friends I have ever known
    I find it the *best* of all.

We rarely meet when the World is near,
    For the World hath a pleasing art,
And brings me so much that is bright and dear
    That my Soul it keepeth apart.

But when I grow weary of mirth and glee,
    Of glitter, glow, and splendour,
Like a tried old friend it comes to me
    With a smile that is sad and tender.

And we walk together as two friends may,
    And laugh, and drink God's wine.
Oh, a royal comrade any day,
    I find this Soul of mine.

"Thus I went wide-where, walking alone"

William Langland

From **THE VISION OF DO-WELL in PIERS PLOWMAN**

Translated from Middle English by Arthur Burrell
(1859–1946)

Thus I went wide-where, walking alone,
In a wide wilderness, by a wood side.
Bliss of the birds song made me abide there,
And on a lawn under a linden I leaned awhile
To listen to their lays, their lovely notes;
The mirth of their mouths made me to sleep,
And mid that bliss I dreamed—marvellously.

Long Island Sound

Emma Lazarus

I see it as it looked one afternoon
In August,—by a fresh soft breeze o'erblown.
The swiftness of the tide, the light thereon,
A far-off sail, white as a crescent moon.
The shining waters with pale currents strewn,
The quiet fishing-smacks, the Eastern cove,
The semi-circle of its dark, green grove.
The luminous grasses, and the merry sun
In the grave sky; the sparkle far and wide,
Laughter of unseen children, cheerful chirp
Of crickets, and low lisp of rippling tide,
Light summer clouds fantastical as sleep
Changing unnoted while I gazed thereon.
All these fair sounds and sights I made my own.

Lyrical Epigrams

Edith Wharton

I
My little old dog:
A heart-beat
At my feet.

II *Spring*
A winter wind,
Primroses,
And the new furrow.

III *Friendship*
The silence of midnight,
A dying fire,
And the best unsaid....

IV
A pointed steeple
Above square trees—
Rustic France.

V
A blunt steeple
Over round trees—
Rural England.

VI *Soluntum*
Across these giant ruins
The greatest cloud-shadows
Dart like little lizards.

Bushland—In the You Yangs

Arthur Patchett Martin

Not sweeter to the storm-tossed mariner
   Is glimpse of home, where wife and children wait
   To welcome him with kisses by the gate,
Than to the town-worn man the breezy stir
   Of mountain winds on rugged pathless heights:
   His long-pent soul drinks in the deep delights
That Nature hath in store. The sun-kissed bay
   Gleams thro' the grand old gnarlèd gum-tree boughs
Like burnished brass; the strong-winged bird of prey
   Sweeps by, upon his lonely vengeful way—
While over all, like breath of holy vows,
   The sweet airs blow, and the high-vaulted sky
   Looks down in pity this fair summer day
   On all poor earth-born creatures doomed to die.

The Awakening River

Katherine Mansfield

The gulls are mad-in-love with the river
And the river unveils her face and smiles.
In her sleep-brooding eyes they mirror their shining
   wings.
She lies on silver pillows: the sun leans over her.
He warms and warms her, he kisses and kisses her.
There are sparks in her hair and she stirs in laughter.
Be careful, my beautiful waking one! You will catch
   on fire.
Wheeling and flying with the foam of the sea on their
   breasts
The ineffable mists of the sea clinging to their wild
   wings
Crying the rapture of the boundless ocean.
The gulls are mad-in-love with the river.
Wake! we are the dream thoughts flying from your
   heart.
Wake! we are the songs of desire flowing from your
   bosom.
O, I think the sun will lend her his great wings
And the river will fly away to the sea with the mad-in-
   love birds.

New Every Morning

Susan Coolidge

Every day is a fresh beginning,
　　Every morn is the world made new.
You who are weary of sorrow and sinning,
　　Here is a beautiful hope for you,—
　　A hope for me and a hope for you.

All the past things are past and over;
　　The tasks are done and the tears are shed.
Yesterday's errors let yesterday cover;
　　Yesterday's wounds, which smarted and bled,
　　Are healed with the healing which night has shed.

Yesterday now is a part of forever,
　　Bound up in a sheaf, which God holds tight,
With glad days, and sad days, and bad days, which
　　never
　　Shall visit us more with their bloom and their blight,
　　Their fulness of sunshine or sorrowful night.

Let them go, since we cannot re-live them,
　　Cannot undo and cannot atone;
God in his mercy receive, forgive them!
　　Only the new days are our own;
　　To-day is ours, and to-day alone.

Here are the skies all burnished brightly,
    Here is the spent earth all re-born,
Here are the tired limbs springing lightly
    To face the sun and to share with the morn
    In the chrism of dew and the cool of dawn.

Every day is a fresh beginning;
    Listen, my soul, to the glad refrain,
And, spite of old sorrow and older sinning,
    And puzzles forecasted and possible pain,
    Take heart with the day, and begin again.

The Cottager to Her Infant

Dorothy Wordsworth

The days are cold, the nights are long,
The north-wind sings a doleful song;
Then hush again upon my breast;
All merry things are now at rest,
　Save thee, my pretty Love!

The kitten sleeps upon the hearth,
The crickets long have ceased their mirth;
There's nothing stirring in the house
Save one *wee*, hungry, nibbling mouse,
　Then why so busy thou?

Nay! start not at the sparkling light;
'Tis but the moon that shines so bright
On the window pane bedropped with rain:
Then, little Darling! sleep again,
　And wake when it is day.

A Noiseless Patient Spider

Walt Whitman

A noiseless patient spider,
I mark'd where on a little promontory it stood isolated,
Mark'd how to explore the vacant vast surrounding,
It launch'd forth filament, filament, filament, out of
    itself,
Ever unreeling them, ever tirelessly speeding them.

And you O my soul where you stand,
Surrounded, detached, in measureless oceans of space,
Ceaselessly musing, venturing, throwing, seeking the
    spheres to connect them,
Till the bridge you will need be form'd, till the ductile
    anchor hold,
Till the gossamer thread you fling catch somewhere,
    O my soul.

Joy

Clarissa Scott Delany

Joy shakes me like the wind that lifts a sail,
Like the roistering wind
That laughs through stalwart pines.
It floods me like the sun
On rain-drenched trees
That flash with silver and green.

I abandon myself to joy—
I laugh—I sing.
Too long have I walked a desolate way,
Too long stumbled down a maze
Bewildered.

The Ocean

Nathaniel Hawthorne

The Ocean has its silent caves,
Deep, quiet and alone;
Though there be fury on the waves,
Beneath them there is none.
The awful spirits of the deep
Hold their communion there;
And there are those for whom we weep,
The young, the bright, the fair.

Calmly the wearied seamen rest
Beneath their own blue sea.
The ocean solitudes are blest,
For there is purity.
The earth has guilt, the earth has care,
Unquiet are its graves;
But peaceful sleep is ever there,
Beneath the dark blue waves.

The Skaters
John Gould Fletcher

Black swallows swooping or gliding,
In a flurry of entangled loops and curves;
The skaters skim over the frozen river.
And the grinding click of their skates as they impinge
    upon the surface
Is like the brushing together of thin wing-tips of silver.

"Nature" is what we see

Emily Dickinson

Nature is what we see,
The Hill, the Afternoon—
Squirrel, Eclipse, the Bumble-bee,
Nay—Nature is Heaven.

Nature is what we hear,
The Bobolink, the Sea—
Thunder, the Cricket—
Nay,—Nature is Harmony.

Nature is what we know
But have no art to say,
So impotent our wisdom is
To Her simplicity.

Sonnet

Alice Moore Dunbar-Nelson

I had not thought of violets late,
The wild, shy kind that spring beneath your feet
In wistful April days, when lovers mate
And wander through the fields in raptures sweet.
The thought of violets meant florists' shops,
And bows and pins, and perfumed papers fine;
And garish lights, and mincing little fops
And cabarets and soaps, and deadening wines.
So far from sweet real things my thoughts had strayed,
I had forgot wide fields; and clear brown streams;
The perfect loveliness that God has made,—
Wild violets shy and Heaven-mounting dreams.
And now—unwittingly, you've made me dream
Of violets, and my soul's forgotten gleam.

[The faint shadow of the morning moon?]

Yone Noguchi

The faint shadow of the morning moon?
Nay, the snow falling on the earth.
The mist of blossoming flowers?
Nay, poetry smiling up the sky.

The Throne of Osiris

Eva Gore-Booth

In the roof the swallow has built her nest,
And the martins under the eaves,
And all wingèd things have a chamber of rest
In the shadow of swaying leaves.

The rabbit has dug for himself a hole,
The green worm lies at the heart of the rose,
And there is rest for the vagrant soul
Wherever the shallowest river flows.

May the Road Rise
Up to Meet You

Traditional Gaelic blessing

May the road rise up to meet you.
May the wind be always at your back.
May the sun shine warm upon your face;
the rains fall soft upon your fields
   and until we meet again,
may God hold you in the palm of His hand.

Songs for the People

Frances Ellen Watkins Harper

Let me make the songs for the people,
  Songs for the old and young;
Songs to stir like a battle-cry
  Wherever they are sung.

Not for the clashing of sabres,
  For carnage nor for strife;
But songs to thrill the hearts of men
  With more abundant life.

Let me make the songs for the weary,
  Amid life's fever and fret,
Till hearts shall relax their tension,
  And careworn brows forget.

Let me sing for little children,
  Before their footsteps stray,
Sweet anthems of love and duty,
  To float o'er life's highway.

I would sing for the poor and aged,
  When shadows dim their sight;
Of the bright and restful mansions,
  Where there shall be no night.

Our world, so worn and weary,
   Needs music, pure and strong,
To hush the jangle and discords
   Of sorrow, pain, and wrong.

Music to soothe all its sorrow,
   Till war and crime shall cease;
And the hearts of men grown tender
   Girdle the world with peace.

Author Biographies

Louisa May Alcott (1832–1888). An American writer best known for her novel *Little Women* and its sequels. *(Page 112)*

Philip James Bailey (1816–1902). A poet from Nottingham, England. Author of *Festus*, a religious work first published anonymously. *(79)*

Aphra Behn (1640–1689). An English poet and playwright. She was one of the first English women to earn her living by writing. *(83)*

William Blake (1757–1827). A poet, painter, and engraver from London who claimed to have visions. *(74, 96)*

Jean Blewett (1862–1934). A Canadian poet of Scottish descent. She began publishing her poetry and stories while she was still a teenager. *(104)*

Anne Brontë (1820–1849). The youngest of the Brontë sisters, and the author of *Agnes Grey* and *The Tenant of Wildfell Hall*. *(99)*

Charlotte Brontë (1816–1855). An English novelist and poet who wrote *Jane Eyre*. She and her sisters Emily and Anne also published a book of poetry together. *(62, 121)*

Emily Brontë (1818–1848). The author of the novel *Wuthering Heights* and a well-regarded poet. *(69)*

Elizabeth Barrett Browning (1806–1861). A popular and acclaimed English poet. She eloped with fellow poet Robert Browning and moved to Italy. *(15)*

Robert Burns (1759–1796). A Scottish poet widely regarded as the Bard of Scotland. Burns Night is celebrated annually on his birthday to honor his life, poetry, and songs. *(10, 64)*

Lewis Carroll (1832–1898). An English writer best known for his book *Alice's Adventures in Wonderland* and his poetry. *(114)*

Willa Cather (1873–1947). An American writer who documented life at the turn of the 20th century on the Great Plains of the Midwest in her novels *O Pioneers!* and *My Ántonia*. *(26)*

John Clare (1793–1864). An English "peasant poet" from Northamptonshire who worked as a farm laborer. Many of his poems were only published after his death. *(52)*

Samuel Taylor Coleridge (1772–1834). An English poet and close friend of William Wordsworth. *(84)*

Susan Coolidge (1835–1905). The pen name of Sarah Chauncey Woolsey. The author of the classic children's novel *What Katy Did*. *(166)*

Clarissa Scott Delany (1901–1927). An American poet and social worker whose work contributed to the Harlem Renaissance. *(67, 170)*

Charles Dickens (1812–1870). A hugely popular and successful English novelist. The author of fifteen novels, including *Oliver Twist* and *A Tale of Two Cities*, as well as the novella *A Christmas Carol*. *(128)*

Emily Dickinson (1830–1886). She lived all her life in Amherst, Massachusetts, in increasing seclusion. She was not well-known as a poet in her lifetime, but thousands of her poems were discovered and published after her death. *(12, 37, 68, 90, 155, 173)*

John Donne (1572–1631). An English metaphysical poet and Dean of St Paul's Cathedral in London. *(102)*

Paul Laurence Dunbar (1872–1906). An African American poet and novelist, son of two formerly enslaved people. He published many books and achieved international success. *(21, 48, 157)*

Alice Moore Dunbar-Nelson (1875–1935). Born in New Orleans, Louisiana, she was the daughter of a formerly enslaved African American seamstress and a white merchant marine. She published her first book of poetry at the age of twenty. *(11, 77, 174)*

George Eliot (1819–1880). The pen name of Mary Ann Evans, an English novelist, poet, and translator, renowned for the psychological insight she brought to her characterizations. *(122)*

Queen Elizabeth I (1533–1603). The Queen of England and the last monarch of the Tudor dynasty. She inspired other writers of her time, including William Shakespeare and Edmund Spenser. *(51)*

F. Scott Fitzgerald (1896–1940). An American novelist best known for the iconic novel *The Great Gatsby*, depicting life during the Jazz Age of the 1920s. He also wrote short stories and some poems. *(126)*

James Elroy Flecker (1884–1915). An English novelist, playwright, and poet. *(110, 140)*

John Gould Fletcher (1886–1950). An Imagist poet from Little Rock, Arkansas. His poetry was inspired by art, philosophy, and music. *(172)*

Robert Frost (1874–1963). An American poet well-known for his colloquial language and his depictions of rural New England. *(134)*

Elsa Gidlow (1898–1986). An English poet and journalist credited with publishing the first book of openly lesbian poetry in North America. *(27)*

Eva Gore-Booth (1870–1926). An Irish poet and theologian. She was also a political activist and advocated for all women to have the right to vote. *(156, 176)*

Lady Augusta Gregory (1852–1932). An Anglo-Irish writer and folklorist. She was a key player in the Irish Literary Revival in the late 1800s. *(58)*

Hannah Griffitts (1727–1817). An American writer from Philadelphia, Pennsylvania. She was an avid supporter of the American protest against the British in the run-up to the American Revolution. *(95)*

Frances Ellen Watkins Harper (1825–1911). A poet, author, lecturer, abolitionist, and suffragist. She co-founded the National Association of Colored Women's Clubs. She was the first African American woman to publish a short story. *(178)*

Nathaniel Hawthorne (1804–1864). The author of the classic American novel *The Scarlet Letter. (171)*

William Ernest Henley (1849–1903). An English poet. He started writing poetry at the age of twelve while recovering from surgery. *(103)*

Gerard Manley Hopkins (1844–1889). An English poet and Jesuit priest. Most of his poetry was published many years after his death. *(50)*

Langston Hughes (1901–1967). An American poet, novelist, playwright, and activist. He pioneered jazz poetry and was a leading voice in the Harlem Renaissance. *(47, 132)*

James Weldon Johnson (1871–1938). An American writer and civil rights activist. *(154)*

Ellen Johnston (c. 1835–1874). Also known as "The Factory Girl," she was a Scottish power-loom weaver and poet. *(54)*

Charles Lamb (1775–1834) and Mary Lamb (1764–1847). They were siblings and writers. They collaborated on *Tales from Shakespeare*. *(82)*

Letitia Elizabeth Landon (1802–1838). An English poet and novelist, often known as L.E.L. *(92)*

William Langland (c. 1330–1400). The author of the Middle English poem "Piers Plowman." *(160)*

D. H. Lawrence (1885–1930). An English novelist and poet. His novel *Lady Chatterley's Lover* was subject to an obscenity trial in 1960 and was even banned in some countries. *(34)*

Emma Lazarus (1849–1887). A Jewish American poet whose sonnet "The New Colossus" is inscribed on the pedestal of the Statue of Liberty. *(161)*

Henry Wadsworth Longfellow (1807–1882). A prolific American poet from New England, known as one of the fireside poets. The author of the epic poem *The Song of Hiawatha*. *(117)*

Amy Lowell (1874–1925). An American poet from New England. She wrote in the Imagist style. *(22, 75, 118)*

Edward Robert Bulwer-Lytton (1831–1891). An English writer and politician. He published poems under the pen name Owen Meredith. *(61)*

Katherine Mansfield (1888–1923). A New Zealand short story writer and poet. Her poems often focused on finding the beauty in ordinary things. *(31, 165)*

Arthur Patchett Martin (1851–1902). An Australian writer who worked as a journalist and literary critic. *(164)*

Edgar Lee Masters (1868–1950). He is best known for the *Spoon River Anthology*, which contains free verse poems on rural and small-town American life. *(94)*

Claude McKay (1889–1948). Born in Jamaica, McKay was a key figure of the Harlem Renaissance. He became an American citizen in 1940. *(16, 33, 98, 138)*

Herman Melville (1819–1891). An American novelist, short-story writer, and poet. The author of *Moby Dick*, the story of a whale-hunting voyage. *(116)*

Charlotte Mew (1869–1928). An English poet from London who struggled with mental illness and loneliness. Her poetry achieved critical acclaim. *(136)*

Alice Meynell (1847–1922). An English writer and campaigner for women's rights. *(45)*

Edna St. Vincent Millay (1892–1950). A major twentieth-century American lyrical poet. She was known for her riveting readings of her poetry. *(40, 46)*

John Milton (1608–1674). A seventeenth-century English poet. The author of *Paradise Lost*, telling the biblical story of the *Fall of Man*. He continued to write by dictation after losing his eyesight. *(20, 106)*

Lucy Maud Montgomery (1874–1942). A writer from Prince Edward Island, Canada. The author of the *Anne of Green Gables* stories. *(30, 78)*

E. Nesbit (1858–1924). An English writer and poet. The author of children's classic *The Railway Children*. *(91)*

Yone Noguchi (1875–1947). A Japanese novelist, poet, critic, and essayist, he is cited as the first Japanese writer to publish poems in English and is the father of famous sculptor Isamu Noguchi. *(175)*

Arthur O'Shaughnessy (1844–1881). An English poet of Irish descent, born in London. He worked at the British Museum in the Zoology Department. *(111)*

Dorothy Parker (1893–1967). An American writer, critic, and satirist celebrated for her humor and wit. *(44)*

Edgar Allan Poe (1809–1849). An American poet and short story writer from Boston, Massachusetts. He wrote using themes of mystery and the macabre. *(60, 123, 142)*

Francis Quarles (1592–1644). An English poet from Essex. His family had served the royal family for generations. *(70)*

Ameen Rihani (1876–1940). A Lebanese American writer and activist who participated in the mahjar literary movement, a migration of Syrian and Lebanese romantic poets to the Americas. *(66)*

George Roberts (1873–1953). An Irish poet and actor. He co-founded a publishing house which printed works that became part of the Irish Literary Revival. *(41)*

Christina Rossetti (1830–1894). An extremely well-regarded English poet of the Victorian era. The sister of Dante Gabriel Rossetti. *(19, 42)*

Dante Gabriel Rossetti (1828–1882). An English poet and painter. The brother of poet Christina Rossetti. *(139)*

Sappho (c. 610–750 BCE). A Greek poet whose works survive only in fragments. She is considered one of the greatest lyric poets of antiquity. *(139)*

Sir Walter Scott (1771–1832). A prolific and hugely popular Scottish writer from Edinburgh. *(18)*

William Shakespeare (1564–1616). An English playwright, poet, and actor who is often regarded as the greatest writer in the English language. The author of *Romeo and Juliet, Macbeth*, and many other plays. *(14, 36, 76)*

Mary Wollstonecraft Shelley (1797–1851). An English novelist best known for her gothic novel *Frankenstein*.

The daughter of early feminist Mary Wollstonecraft and wife of poet Percy Bysshe Shelley. *(32)*

Sir Philip Sidney (1554–1586). An English poet, scholar, soldier, and courtier of the Elizabethan court. *(23)*

Edmund Spenser (1552–1599). An English poet, writing during the reign of Queen Elizabeth I. The author of the epic poem *The Faerie Queene. (24)*

Sara Teasdale (1884–1933). An American lyric poet. Born in St. Louis, Missouri, she moved to New York City in 1916. *(17, 25, 35, 53, 71, 152)*

Henry David Thoreau (1817–1862). An American philosopher, poet, and environmental thinker. The author of *Walden; or, Life in the Woods*, an account of living a simple life in a cabin. *(28)*

Edith Wharton (1862–1937). Born in New York, she was the first woman to win the Pulitzer Prize in Fiction for her novel *The Age of Innocence*, portraying the lives of the upper classes in the 1920s. *(162)*

Phillis Wheatley (1753–1784). An enslaved person who became the first African American author to have a book of poetry published. *(120)*

Walt Whitman (1819–1892). One of the most influential poets in American literature. As a teenager, he founded his own newspaper. *(169)*

Ella Wheeler Wilcox (1850–1919). An American poet and journalist. *(158)*

Oscar Wilde (1854–1900). A poet and dramatist from Dublin, Ireland. An advocate of art for art's sake. Wilde was imprisoned for two years when homosexuality was a crime in Britain. *(80)*

Virginia Woolf (1882–1941). Part of the Bloomsbury Set, a group of English writers. Her novels used the stream-of-consciousness technique. *(153)*

Dorothy Wordsworth (1771–1855). The sister of William Wordsworth and the author of well-regarded diaries that were published after her death. *(168)*

William Wordsworth (1770–1850). One of the English Lake poets, he wrote about the relationship between people and nature. *(130)*

Sir Thomas Wyatt (1503–1542). An English poet, politician, and ambassador. He was briefly imprisoned in the Tower of London for allegedly committing adultery with Anne Boleyn. *(56)*

W. B. Yeats (1865–1939). One of the greatest Irish poets of the 20th century. *(124)*

A Playlist for Tortured Souls

Artists, musicians, and poets inspire us—and one another. Their works often share themes and imagery, and the poems in this collection might hit different when paired with a Taylor Swift song. Here is a starter playlist for each section, highlighting just some of the many songs that can live in conversation with the poetry.

Love

"evermore"

"Love Story"

"Lover"

Pair with "One Sister have I in our house" by Emily Dickinson (page 12)

Heartache

"All Too Well"

"The Black Dog"

"Dear John"

Pair with "I shot the ALBATROSS" by Samuel Taylor Coleridge (page 84)

Pair with "Her First Sorrow" by Ameen Rihani (page 66)

Revenge

"Look What You Made Me Do"

"The Albatross"

"Who's Afraid of Little Old Me?"

Folklore

"Wonderland"

"So Long, London"

"the lakes"

Pair with "Comrades" by Ella Wheeler Wilcox (page 158)

Pair with "A Boat, Beneath a Sunny Sky" by Lewis Carroll (page 114)

Peace

"You're On Your Own, Kid"

"invisible string"

"You Are In Love"

.